THE SHAMAN'S QUEST

Norman W. Wilson PhD

THE SHAMAN'S QUEST

Cover Design by

www.srwalkerdesigns.com

A ZADKIEL PUBLISHING PAPERBACK

© Copyright 2018
Norman W. Wilson PhD

The right of Norman W. Wilson to be identified as author and channel of this work has been asserted by him in accordance with the Copyright, Designs and Patents Act 1988.

All Rights Reserved

No reproduction, copy or transmission of the publication may be made without written permission.

No paragraph of this publication may be reproduced, copied or transmitted save with the written permission of the publisher, or in accordance with the provisions of the Copyright Act 1956 (as amended).

Any person who does any unauthorised act in relation to this publication may be liable to criminal prosecution and civil claims for damages.

ISBN: 978-1-78695-169-4

Zadkiel Publishing
An Imprint of Fiction4All
www.fiction4all.com

This Edition
Published 2018

The genuine seeker is one who has a "constant and passionate longing to break free from life's sorrows—not by running away from it, but by growing beyond his mind and by experiencing in himself the reality of the Self which knows neither birth nor death."

Sage Ramana Maharshi

ACKNOWLEDGMENTS

I am indebted to several wonderful people for their help, support, and encouragement as I struggled to bring these conversations together in a rational and coherent presentation. Much of the material here is based upon conversations the author had with his own personal mentor, Strato E Telvely.

I owe a debt of thanks to Merle Benda, an outstanding bowman. His input on elk hunting, the use of bow and arrow, and the culture of the elk people have been invaluable in helping me bring long lost memories and an authenticity to this book.

Suzanne deserves a special note of appreciation for her patience and understanding as I ignored her by spending so much time at the computer.

A very special note of appreciation to Bernard Jerome, Cultural Development Director, Aroostook Band of Mik'Maqs, Presque Isle, Maine for his assistance in tracking down specific ingredients in Mik'Maq medicines.

A huge thanks goes to Scott Huot of Montreal for his transformation of my original manuscript into a PDF file as well as into an HTML document.

To Stephen R Walker of S.R. Walker Designs, Atlanta, for his tireless help in designing the cover and back cover for my novel.

I am still awed by this marvelous technology we call The Internet, and the vast resources it has made available from the comfort of my office. It has saved me thousands of hours in the stacks of multiple libraries scattered across our country.

Last, but not least, a thank you to my publisher, Stuart Holland, at Zadkiel Publishing.

Finally, I am appreciative of my own being. I have been privy to so much.

NWW
Camano Island
2018

DEDICATION

For the Seeker in all of us; whomever we may be.

DEDICATION

To the Seeker in all of us in hopes we never stop questioning...

AUTHOR'S NOTE

The original concept for this book came about during many afternoon discussion with my friend and mentor, the late Strato E. Telvely, a true Renaissance man. He was a former school superintendent who became my life-long friend. I would get home from teaching at a local college around 1:00 o'clock in the afternoon. He would arrive for coffee and an afternoon discussion of a wide variety of esoteric topics ranging from philosophy, music, art, literature, ancient history, psychology, and education. Politics was not on the agenda. As he would say, "We have time for another piece of cake and another cup of coffee and then we'll talk some more." Maybe around the tenth week of these discussions I realized I should be taking notes.

Eventually, those notes turned into a book called The Quest: Seeking the New Adam published in 2000. The method of narration was, of course, a discussion between and older man and a younger man. I eventually, realized that the book really needed serious revision. It needed a real plot, character development, action, and description. Otherwise, it was a mess.

Slowly, and painfully so, The Shaman's Quest emerged as I built personal experience into the book, provided a philosophical underpinning for the characters, and developed my mentor into a First

Nation healer, one I would call Esaugetuh, the Master of Breath.

The current version is a refinement of the original. I have attempted to tweak the two main characters, added a few minor characters, and to lay the basis for a series of books with the same main characters. I kept the name Adam, meaning original man or man of the earth.

CHAPTER ONE
THE SEEKER

The nature of the sacred quest is such that you may have a word, name, or concept of what it is you are looking for, some idea of what it is, how and where it may be found.

Tau Malachi
(*The Gnostic Gospel of St. Thomas*)

Often, as it was in my case, I couldn't put a handle on what I was looking for. For me, the mystery began when I was a kid traveling into the backcountry of the Eastern Canadian bush with my parents.

My father, actually I don't remember of ever calling him that or calling him pop or dad or anything, would pack a large trailer full of supplies, including two toys and two of my favorite books for me. I was also allowed a note book and a couple of pencils and a sharpener. I could have one book in the Buick.

Fishing gear, life jackets, boat cushions, a twenty-five horse Johnson outboard motor, cans for gasoline, and cans for kerosene got stashed along the sides of a gigantic ice chest that sat over the middle axel of the trailer. He'd had it made special as well as the trailer.

Everything had to be balanced just so. I guess he viewed life that way. There had to be meat, potatoes even though he did not view potatoes as a vegetable, and two vegetables on his plate. Balanced. A fishing lure had to have two sets of hooks, no singles, or threes; one set in front and one at the rear of the lure. Spinners were the exception. The three pronged hook was always at the rear. His office desk was balanced: telephone on the right, a family photo on the left, pen set in the center.

The ice chest which held such a prestigious position was packed with food: flour, salt, pepper, sugar, coffee, pasta, and dozens of other consumable items. Fresh stuff was bought at the last small town some fifty miles before hitting the off road to the lake and our camp. A pillow, blanket, snacks, and a thermos of coffee went in the car. Clothes were packed in the trunk, enough for two to three months.

We headed out at about three in the morning because my father liked to get an early start. We were heading into northwestern Quebec Province where we would spend the summer on a large lake with a group Indians who camped there. It was a sixteen hour trip, with stops only to gas up, and to eat one meal while on the road. If I had to pee he pulled off to the side of the road. As soon as we got there, he would nap for an hour and then unload the trailer, and go fishing. He seemed drawn to the water, needing it to nourish him. Strange I never thought of it that way then, but now is now and things are different.

It was his way of getting away from it all. No telephones ringing, no radios. No one at the office to pester him with questions about commodities. No parties and dinners with insufferable people. Whatever it was, that attracted him to the lake it seemed to pull him further into himself. It was during those times that my mother would take long walks into the woods and sometimes the two of us would visit one of the teepees. Much of the time I was left to explore my version of the world.

Living in a one-room log cabin with a dirt floor, a legless cast-iron pot-bellied stove, and one window covered with cheese-cloth was just the right setting for an adventurous seven year old, well to be seven in a couple of months. Two beds, actually wooden poles driven into the earthen floor with scrapped moose skin drawn tight for the mattresses, lined up against the two side walls of the cabin. The stove sat in the middle of the room, a small handmade wooden table sat beneath the lone window. An old wooden chair sat at each end. In the middle was a cut log, about 24 inches high when standing on its end. That was for me to sit on. An old rocking chair was near the stove. My mother called it a Boston rocker.

Since there was no electricity, kerosene lamps were lit when it got dark. It was my job to go into the woods to a natural spring with a tin bucket for our drinking water. Once the water bugs and mosquitoes were dispensed with, I would scoop up the water, and slosh it back to the cabin. That was my daily chore. And since there was no running water, there was no inside toilet. There was the "out house." Fortunately one of the items packed was toilet paper.

Besides hearing the wolves running during the night, the occasional bear using the side of the cabin as a back-scratcher, and the grunts and heavy breathing that sometimes came from my parents' bed, a few other things still remain clear in my mind. One was the fact that the Indians had no children. I suppose that made me a curiosity. Another was the whispering among the squaws who pretended I wasn't there whenever I ventured up to one of their teepees. And finally, there was an episode involving my father that particularly stands out in memory.

He and I seldom had anything to say to one another. As I said earlier, I never made reference to him as dad or pop. I always remained at a polite and discrete distance both physically and psychologically. I think by the time I was four I stopped wondering about it even though I noticed how other boys and their fathers behaved toward one another. I used to wish he'd pick me up and carry me high up on his shoulders. He never did, of course. When he did speak to me it was always an order, almost barked. Yet, there was a generosity about him. That certainly sounds like a contradiction if I ever heard of one, but that's what brings me to this other remembrance. It was such a powerful thing, so much so that I can bring it graphically to mind with ease. It became a great object lesson in my life.

It happened on one of the earlier trips we made into the Canadian bush. He had taken me out in the boat fishing. I didn't catch anything but he had a nice catch of Greathnothern Pike. As I scrambled up the sandy embankment to our little log cabin I saw an old Indian woman standing near the cabin. I had not seen her before and wondered who she was.

She was a mess; her tangled white-streaked hair was full of leaves, and her dress was muddy. She began talking and gesturing. Sounded like gibberish to me so I just stood there, too dumb to say anything. Once my father was up the bank and had spotted her, he spoke to her in the same sort of gibberish. He sure seemed to understand. Anyway, he did the darndest thing. He picked out the largest fish, walked over to her, and gave it to her. Immediately she began to gum it. Even though she had no teeth she somehow was able to tear it open and began eating it, guts, and all.

Seeing my concern my father said, "She's been left to die. The others of her tribe have moved on. She's too old and sickly to travel with them."

"Why?" I whispered.

"It's her duty to stay behind."

"Why'd you give her food?"

" No more questions!"

Her duty to die? I wondered about that. I thought everyone was to live life to the fullest, whatever that meant. And from Bible School, I remembered they added the statement, 'to serve others.'

At the time I thought it was the cruelest thing I had ever heard of—not realizing, of course, that I was passing judgment on a culture that had a different set of values than mine. Today I consider such judgment pretentious.

Later that night, after he had had his evening glass of whiskey, I mustered up the courage to dare ask him another question, "What are those Indian women always whispering about? Every time I go near them they start to whisper. Isn't that rude?"

"Some high mucky muck of a medicine man. Seems he disappeared right in front of their eyes. If you ask me, it was simply too much of that cheap rot gut they drink."

"Did you ever see him?"

"Enough questions!"

It was always that way. I always had more questions than I had answers. We finally stopped making the sojourn into the backwoods when I was in my late teens but every summer that we were there I asked about the mysterious medicine man the old ones whispered about, the one who could disappear right in front of your eyes. Gradually through the many trips, I picked up bits and pieces of information.

A dropped comment was always fodder for more questions and like precious pieces of gold, they had become something for me to treasure. With meticulous care I jotted these treasures in my note books. Even some of my college texts had little comments in the margins of their pages. Of course, I had no idea at the time that this disappearing Indian medicine man would become the driving force in my existence, the center for my quest. Actually the external representation of my quest.

One thing was for sure, I was battling heavy eyes, and it was a losing battle. Flashes of yellow lightening raced across the darkened sky providing glimpses of strangely shaped clouds. I wondered if I was driving into a twister. The rain finally came. An unbelievable downpour so intense that the headlights of cars on the interstate were nothing more than vague patches of blurred yellow that shot phantom-like off into the night. Catching myself nodding, I hit the brakes. Fortunately, they were antilock or I would have slid into the guard rail. I realized I was very close to an exit so with a quick jerk on the steering wheel I shot down the off ramp. I wasn't sure exactly where I was other than somewhere in central Florida.

Creeping along at a snail's pace I spotted a mom and pop motel and pulled in.

Damn! Wouldn't you know? Closed.

Anyway, I figured it to be as good a place as any to park and get some much needed sleep. The trip down from northeastern Canada took more out of me than I had figured. My six foot body wedded to the car seat begged for respite.

I had been driving south for what seemed an eternity besides that I was hungry and pissed. No success in finding the ever elusive medicine man.

Man! Most guys my age have married, knocked out a couple of kids, and are working nine to five. And me, well, I guess you could say I'm still making the chase. What the hell for? Don't I have a good job in New York? And what about Jacquelyn? I can't ask for a better woman. She's always there for me, whenever I need her. Need her? Is that my idea or hers? Saturday morning tennis and Sunday afternoon golf. Early every Wednesday morning it was workout at the gym. Then there were the

Sunday dinners, either at her folks or at mine. That's the problem. Everything was so lack-luster, a smear of one day passing into another. Lack luster is a bit strong. Don't get me wrong. There were good times, fun, laughter, and moments of intimacy. There just wasn't any change in the endless cycle of our daily lives and relationship.

I guess what really bothered me was the fact that no one in my family or Jacquelyn, or friends were sincerely interested in my questions or even concerned that I had them. And they weren't all about my mysterious medicine man. No one seemed to be able to answer my most basic questions and believe me, I had a lot of them. Why do we hate? How's that one? Oh, man, I got a real pile of shit handed down on that one, but no real answer. Priests, rabbis, gurus, or university philosophy and psychology professors could not provide the answers I so desperately wanted—no— needed!

I felt that somehow since I wasn't' getting answers, I had to find a cure for this damnable everlasting gnawing in my gut. I was sure that there was something more, that there was some secret that I should know, some eternal, pregnant secret. I felt I was being haunted. And I was just as sure, if I didn't find answers, I would go insane.

Oh sure, as a kid I always had to know, but that was typical kid behavior. Unfortunately, it carried over into my adult life. I remember my old man used to say, "That boy needs to know the asshole of everything." It wasn't until I was in my teens that I understood the full intent of his comment. Dogs sniff one another's butts. Had he been near me when I realized that, I'm sure I would have punched him out.

I had been in Canada doing research for a piece I was doing for one of the New York magazines that specialized in alternative medicine. I'm what you call a freelancer; selling research and sometimes actual articles to magazines. Often I complied data for insurance companies, stock brokers, and investment companies. I had not forgotten my Indian medicine man and I had hoped that I could find him, do a piece on native medicine, and get some answers to my questions along the way.

A nagging suspicion that he was more than a medicine man was reinforced by some of the indications that I had had from the Mik'Maq. Perhaps my mysterious medicine man was the god, Glooscap in human form. That would surely be splashed as the headlines of the *New York Times.* Anyway, my research had not gone well. Whoever or whatever he was, leads about him disappeared. Any discussion of a Mik'Maq shaman just dried up. Sure wasn't much different than when I was a kid, and like then, I wasn't sure why people wouldn't talk to me about him. By now he had become *my* shaman and it was very personal.

It was my understanding that a rare few of the Mik'Maq developed certain innate abilities that allowed them to surpass all others in their perceptions, skills, and talents. I suspect they had been able to fine tune their ability to tie into the nonlocal mind. Such persons, as do people do today, had to pay a high price for being different. Those that were power-given were separated from the rest of the village, often living in deep forested areas, isolated and feared. They came back into the village to seek a mate or for sacred rituals they were expected to perform or to provide some of their 'magic' to heal a sick person. The medicine man, renamed by others as shaman, despite being shunned and forced to live outside of the village's daily social activities, was a very important person to the tribe. The one I have been looking for was said to be the last of the most powerful of the shaman— one who knows all things, capable of making miracles—the seventh of the seventh of the seventh.

Rumor had it that this man could come and go at will; that he traveled in a different dimension in different times. If all of this was true, perhaps he really was Glooscap. Christians don't have a lock on the idea of a divinity coming to earth in human form. Okay, I admit I had gone to northeastern Canada in search of this last shaman hoping against hope to be able to spend time with him, that is, if he would let me. I had heard talk that he was antisocial and had a deep distrust of whites. My information, scarce as it was, was that he had gone to Florida to meet with some of the Creeks. No one seemed to know why. They just indicated that I should go south. And here I am.

CHAPTER TWO
THE OLD MAN

Follow toward whom your thoughts bend, with your thoughts following them, this you shall always live.
Zuni prayer

I wasn't sure of the exact time when I became aware that someone was knocking on my car window. My eyes struggled to open as my brain groped to identify some sense of my bearings. As difficult as it was I finally realized that I was staring into the most extraordinary pair of eyes that I had ever seen—penetrating Aryan blue eyes. And my god, I felt their gaze deep into my soul. A shiver played tag along my spine; yet, I had sensed no immediate danger despite the feeling of having been scanned. Forcing myself into wakefulness, a quick survey told me I was still at the mom and pop motel and that those extraordinary blue eyes belonged to an old man with long flowing shimmering white hair.

"Breakfast's ready."

That was all he said. My hunger from the night before reared its head and reminded me that it was still there and was badly in need of appeasement. I heaved myself out of the rental, my nose telling me the direction to go. Inside, a small seven stool counter, steaming coffee, and a mile high stack of cakes waited for me and the smells of bacon and eggs drifted in from the grill. No doubt about it. I was hungry.

"Over easy, right and no lace?"

"Uh, sure. That's great," I said, wondering how he knew I liked my eggs over easy and no lace.

What the hell! I polished off the whole stack of cakes, three eggs, a double rasher of bacon, and four cups of coffee. During my eating frenzy, the old man said nothing,

Strange, I thought, usually, these old farts have—,

"You've come far," he said.

It wasn't' a question; just a statement.

"Yes," I replied.

"Guess you'll want a place to stay. Take the second cabin on the left. Number four. The key's on the peg by the door. Help yourself to the coffee."

With that said, he disappeared through a faded blue-curtained doorway. How'd he know I'd want to stay here? Did I show the need for rest that much? His eyes unnerved me a little. I guess the fact that they weren't threatening threatened me. Yet I was drawn to him, magnet like.

"Guess I better ask him about—,"

"The room's forty a night. Breakfast's three," he said, sticking his head back through the curtained doorway. Particles of dust floated lazily around the curtain as the morning sunlight came in through the one open window. It was obvious that it had been a long time since things had been really cleaned. As with the old places in Florida, there was a musty smell.

After signing in, I picked up the key to cabin number four. It was a short walk down a grassy path that was generously sprinkled with sand spurs, and some kind of multi-colored flower. I let myself in, too tired to unpack, I flopped down on the bed. Its musty smell seemed to penetrate my whole body. Like the place, I suddenly felt very old.

Trying to follow-up the leads about the shaman left me exhausted. The backpacking was bad enough, but portage with the canoe through dense woods from one stream to another and then from lake to lake took its toll. Despite my tiredness, sleep was fitful. Strange swirling images, flashes of intense light intermingled with dark shadows haunted my being. At some point, I remember rolling over and groaning. A knock and his voice wakened me from my uncomfortable slumber. As I rolled off the smelly bed I realized I was soaking wet.

"Man! What the hell's wrong with me?"

"You figure on sleeping your life away? It's past twelve," he said.

"Noon already?"

"No. Midnight," his voice seemed to be an echo. "If you want, come by and I'll feed you even if the grill's closed. Say, you all right in there?"

"Yeah. I'm okay."

As I heard him begin to shuffle away I called out, "Hey! Thanks. Sorry about the hour. Sure would appreciate some food if it's not a problem."

"Come along when you're ready."

I couldn't believe I had slept the whole damn day and half the night. Wasn't like me. True I had been on the road for nearly forty hours, but hell, that was no big deal. A couple hours of sleep always revved up my motor. I don't get it. I'm in good shape, best shape I've been in since my days as a hot athlete in high school. Now wonder what made me think of that? My old man never came to a game. Damn, I'm sure being weird.

A warm breeze blew in from the Gulf. It picked up the smell of sweet Jasmine and I felt better. A couple of possums scurried across the path as I strolled along to the little café that was part of the motel office. I suspected he lived in a back room. Anyway, he watched me devour a 14 ounce steak, the most fabulous steak I had ever eaten in my life, a life of restaurant steaks burnt, raw or dripping in grease, tough, old, or smelly. You name it, I've eaten it. When I finished he shoved a snifter of brandy in front of me.

"Good for what ails you," he said. And that was the first he had spoken since I came in to eat.

He pulled out an old hand made clay pipe, packed it, lit it and eased a draw. He leveled those blue eyes at me as small circles, slowly growing larger, spiraled toward the ceiling. Its aroma was very pleasant. He took no food or drink. He waited for me to take my first sip of the brandy. Its nutty flavor was most enjoyable as I rolled it over my tongue.

"So you have questions," he said.

Again it was a statement.

"Questions you want answered," he continued.

"Well, sure. Doesn't everybody?"

"No. Fools don't. Those who claim wisdom, prophets, and fakirs don't. They pretend to have all the answers. They don't even know the right questions to ask. Do you? Do you know what it is that gnaws at your gut? You don't do you? What a shame because what you seek you already have, you already are. You young ones are never satisfied, are you? One day you wake up and realize all that you had is gone. Gone! And then it's too late."

More smoke rings unfurled from his clay pipe. I was unaware he had taken another puff. I would learn that those smoke rings would signal agitation among other things.

"What's that you are smoking? The aroma's different."

"Kinnikinnick." [1]

"What?"

"It's Algonquian. Means 'smoking mixture.' Your question is about the ultimate, isn't it and your relationship to that ultimate?"

"Well, yes and no. What I want to know, is man, am I, for example—,"

"Begotten of the universe or are you some separate entity, isolated from that which is," he interrupted.

The smoke rings seemed to rush up from the bowl of his clay pipe. Faster than before.

Continuing he said, "Of course man is of the universe. Like it, he came out of the great nothingness—that great swirling cosmic soup that existed before all things. And because he is, there is an interaction, an interconnection between all parts of that universe and him. A wonderful organic living dance, an intercourse. You cannot be discounted as an integral part of its being as you would have it."

"As I would have it? Why do you say that? You say I want to be disconnected? You don't know me." I felt the color seep into my face.

"I'm speaking generally, not of you personally. But now that you have mentioned it." He said as his blue eyes flashed. "Well, you get connected through unity. It's only through unity that you can comprehend anything let alone the ultimate. There has to be a unity of body and Self with the *will* of the universe. Humph! Thought you would have learned that by now. You are disconnected."

"What you're saying is that man is still the consummate seeker—seeking the infinite—always seeking the ultimate, and by that you mean that unifying principle, that which holds all together? Like Einstein?" I said.

"Well, not so much Einstein. More than that, I think. Man seeks as it's his destiny to do but he fails to realize he must do so synoptically. Even as the restless wind seeks the Four Corners from which to spread itself over earth's entire domain, so too, man must seek the sweetest fruit of all, that perfection, that fruition of the expectant eternal universality, that which unifies everything—fecundity. And as in the case of Tantalus [2], it always seems just out of his reach."

"But a finite intellect cannot, by means of comparison, reach an absolute truth. Come on now, you don't expect me to believe that?" I said, proud of myself for not falling into his clever little trap.

"Wrong. Totally wrong!"

"Wrong? How so?" I said.

"First of all, you assumed that the mind is finite. Why should it be? Look, through the use extended metaphor, man grapples with the absolute but only a select few find it. Others try to create it through religion, philosophy, or social institution. Man travels to the outer reaches of the universe through his literature and now through his sciences. Remember, one number always follows another. There is no end. *He* even creates the numbers."

"Are you suggesting that man can transcend to the very level of universality and that when he does, he then, is himself ultimate? Good god! You can't be serious!" I said, blown away by the whole implication.

"Leonardo da Vinci touched on this when he wrote, 'the lover is drawn to the thing loved; and the sense of that by which he perceives, and unites with it, and they become one and the same thing.'"

"Thus, a joining—Nirvana?" I asked.

"No, not Nirvana—fecundity! The reproduction of *Self.* Every part is contained in the universe, in the whole. Division replicates the whole as does a piece of holographic film contain all that the whole contained."

"Then accordingly, what you are saying is that images of objects are spread throughout the air which surrounds them is true? Even throughout the universe itself, much like that stinking smoke from your pipe," I snapped.

I don't know why I am annoyed. The smoke certainly didn't stink. It was just something I couldn't put a finger on. What annoyed me even more was the fact that he knew it. And why that should bother me I hadn't the foggiest idea. Anyway, after a long pause, he took a drag on his pipe, longer than before, and slowly exhaled.

Breaking the killing silence he said, "Look at the rings. They are concentric, floating upwards and outwards becoming a part of the whole until they no longer can be individually identified."

"Okay. I get it. It's the old drop of water in a bucket of water routine. You can't identify the drop from the rest of the water in the bucket," I replied."

"The images of our spheres enter and pass together with all other bodies through a natural point at which time they merge and become united—a whole. That is, they are one and the same. Actually, it's not much different than the Hindu concept of avatar [3]," he said, tapping his pipe on the counter.

"Oh, great! Come on! Who's going to believe that bullshit? It smacks of *New Age* phoniness. Some guru claptrap out of the 1960's," I said.

"You are! You are going to believe it."

"Holy shit! You think I'm a fool?" I shot back.

"At the moment, yes. A story from the old literature will illustrate my point. A man found a butterfly's cocoon and noted that it had a very small opening at one end. Holding the cocoon in his hand he watched as the emerging butterfly struggled to force its body through the little opening. Then it seemed to give up the struggle. The man watched. There was no movement. Using a small knife he made a small slit near the opening. The butterfly emerged easily but not as the man had expected. Its body was swollen and its wings were shriveled. The man continued to watch, expecting its wings to enlarge, waiting for it to take its first solo flight. Neither happened! The butterfly spent the rest of its life crawling around with its swollen body and shriveled wings. You see it was necessary for the butterfly to struggle to get through the small opening to force the fluids from its body into its wings so that they would be ready for flight once it had gained its freedom. Sometimes struggles are needed in our lives to make us strong enough to survive. Otherwise, we'd wither and die. Your problem is you want someone to make an extra slit in your cocoon from which you can emerge."

I sat there stunned. Blown-away.

"I'm tired. Go to bed!" He ordered, disappearing behind the curtained doorway.

Frustrated, angry, and humiliated, I continued to sit there. Pissed mostly at myself. Even my father had stopped ordering me around and here I am in some god forsaken motel letting some old geezer boss me around as if I were a little kid. A dove cooed reminding me that it was fast becoming morning. Off in the distance, a blue jay squawked the morning feeding alarm. I went outside.

The jay's alarm had been picked up by loud mouthed crows. It was a typical early spring morning in Florida. Streaks of orange gold stretched lazily across the sky, highlighted by left over darkened nightshades. A stray cat, from nowhere, in particular, rubbed its head against my leg. I looked down as it curled its tail around my leg. It looked up at me and yawned. It was a good reminder that it was indeed time for me to go to bed.

"Tomorrow, I'll show him who's the fool."

CHAPTER THREE
ONENESS

We are all members of one another.
Saint
Paul

The stillness told me it was late afternoon. By the feel of it probably an afternoon shower was about to break. Typical for Florida. I enjoyed my short stroll to the office-café. Once inside I found no one around and there was no other guests milling about. Looking out the small latticed window of the café, I casually looked down the row of seven cabins. I thought it strange that there wasn't any activity. No maids cleaning rooms and there are always maids cleaning rooms. Taking a closer look at the first cabin I noticed its lone window was boarded up and I could see that the window of the second cabin was boarded up. The place spooked me.

I decided to get the hell out of here. According to a bullet ridden road sign, the nearest town was but a few miles from the motel. I needed gas and a few personals. It sure wasn't much of a town. Crossroads would be a better description. The gas station was the local store, bar, and post office. Houses, more like shacks, were sparse. A couple of young Mexicans in a beat up old truck were ahead of me. Empty crates sat on its flat bed. I assumed they were migrant workers.

There were only two pumps and since the truck took up one side of both pumps I pulled around, coming up on the opposite side. A man was sitting on the steps of the entrance to the bar, bent over in a slumber. Probably sleeping one off. A short squat burly man came out of the bar with a six pack under his arm. Just as he got into his truck he paused and looked directly at me. Usually, I don't feel intimidated but for a moment I thought he spent a little too much time checking me out. I was about to begin pumping gas when a man probably in his mid-fifties came out to pump the gas. No self-service here.

"Fill'er up?"

"Yes. By the way, do you know the owner of the Crosswinds Motel?" I asked.

"You interested in buying that old place? Sure needs a lot of work."

"No. I'm staying out there."

"Didn't know anybody was out there. Been closed for years."

The hair on the nape of my neck curled as a vision of the classic movie, *Psycho* flashed through my mind. "No way am I going back there even if I do owe that old fart a night's lodging and two meals," I thought as I followed the man into the grocery to pay my bill and pick up a couple of items.

Didn't have much in the way of food items, mostly Mexican, lots of cheap wine, a cooler full of beer. No tooth paste or dental floss. I noticed a box of baking soda and bought that. We used to clean our teeth with baking soda while we were in Canada at the log cabin. It worked. I didn't care how it tasted.

I guess I had driven about ten miles when I realized I had made a U-turn and was headed back to the Crosswinds Motel. Swamp cabbage, palmetto, and scrubby evergreens dotted the road side. An occasional cow munched its way along a sagging old rusty fence. No groves here with their neat rows of orange or grapefruit trees. The winding two-lane road had its share of pot holes. No lead-foot possible here. A broken axel would be all I needed. The thought made me shudder. As the road smoothed out I began to whistle. My mood had changed. As I pulled into the entrance, the sun had begun its westward descent promising a beautiful sunset. He was standing in the doorway of the office-café.

His white hair was pulled back and hung in a pony-tail. For a moment I thought I detected a smile beginning on his weathered face. He was a tall as I was, maybe a tad taller, broad shouldered. He was dressed in blue jeans, a white Guayaberas shirt, and leather moccasins. Funny I didn't remember what he was wearing when I first met him. Guess I'm not much of researcher if I can't remember details.

As I approached he said, as if we had been still talking, "Their merger is the only Universality."

"Hold it right there. Merger of what? And next time don't tell me to go to bed, you got that?"

Ignoring my show of assertiveness he continued, "The images of our bodies with other bodies, of course."

Out came the clay pipe, he tapped it on the railing of the small porch of the café. He took his time in filling it, lit it, and drew on it a couple of times.

"You've got to remember that *man* is an integral in nature, space, and time. The Romantics had it all wrong. Man is not a separate entity, separate from nature, something to be held up against nature as a backdrop. It was a foolish effort at determining value. Man is not separate from nature or from the universe itself. What's more, he's multidimensional. Some of the fancier scientists no longer talk about the fourth dimension but now talk, and with a degree of certainty, about ten dimensions. And with projection, we may find there are even more than ten. How is all of this possible? It's possible because of man's relationship to the cosmos. Man is cosmic. Never doubt it!"

The urgency in his voice threw me for a minute as I struggled to ingest all he had said. Finding my voice, I asked, "You mean, when man is one with himself?"

"Yes! Yes! That's it. Isn't all mankind's quest to become one with itself? To know itself? And, my friend, isn't that your quest? Wasn't that Adam's in the Garden of Eden? Wasn't that the real reason Adam ate the 'forbidden fruit' of the tree of knowledge—to know himself as a multidimensional being? And certainly, it was the same for Siddhartha Gautama."

"Wait just a damn minute. Last night you said it was fecundity. Now you are saying it's something different," I said letting my hostility show.

"No! Can't you see that knowing yourself is essential if you are to experience fecundity?"

"Just for the sake of argument, suppose I accept this for the moment. Is it instinctual or is there a deliberate learning-thought process here?"

"We're told that thought has universal field properties which are not unlike gravitational and magnetic field properties. They are amenable." [4]

"How is that possible?"

"Consciousness," he said, looking at me with his penetrating blue eyes.

"Consciousness?"

"Yes. Even though according to some, it may be non-physical, it still may be a real quantity. Look, if science is correct and there are indications that it is, the processes of consciousness in our brain and the subsequent transfers that occur there, in fact, may be due to *quantum mechanical tunneling processes.*"

His baritone voice cracked, dropped several octaves to a near whisper. His face reddened displaying his building agitation. "Shit!" I thought, "if he doesn't' want to answer my questions why in hell did he bring up the goddamn subject to begin with?"

Now I was getting pissed. I yelled, "Damn it. Explain. As far as I'm concerned this is just a bunch of horse shit!"

"You sure are a dumb one. If the organic holograph doesn't have at least three dimensional perceptions to process, it creates its own to perceive, to conceive. Can't you see that? That's fecundity."

"No, I don't see that. Give me a different example. One I can understand."

Losing his sharpness he replied, "Persons who are placed in sensory deprivation chambers begin to hallucinate and synthesize entire inner realities. What we have then, is a kind of yin/yang situation—in nothingness, the ultimate reality begins the hallucinatory process of creation itself. And all this is within the consciousness of the universe."

"How does it work?"

"If the ultimate reality is like a holograph, then human beings are similar to that reality. And if hallucinations are an act of creation, and if the ultimate reality can create/dissolve and recreate-create, then human beings participate in that creation," he said as a hint of a grin fought to come alive at the corner of his lips.

Somehow when he smiled, which was seldom, he looked years younger—almost boyish. It seemed that his eyes became bluer and they opened wider. So much so that they seemed to reach almost to the top of his thick bushy white eyebrows. Not the Groucho Marx eyebrows or the Salvador Dali eyebrows, but rather the kind young Latin men have. The kind that gives them the appearance of all-knowing. Women might interpret them as an open sensual invitation to join him in learning about the art of love. It was that combination that made him disarming.

"How does man do this?" I asked.

With that question, he knew he had me. The hint of the smile broadened into full blossom and as near perfect white teeth filled the space left by smiling lips. A wash of warmth flushed over me. I can't explain it, but somehow, at that moment, in some strange way, I felt I had known this man all of my life. And in spite of that feeling, I'm here up to my neck in some kind of deep shit and I don't even know who it is I'm talking with.

Suddenly I heard myself blurt out, "Who are you? What's your name?"

"Does it matter? What's in a name?" His voice quieted as he continued, "One of your writers expressed it. Carroll? Yes, Lewis Carroll. Smart man that one. It was in his *Alice in Wonderland.* Alice and the knight were talking about the name of a song. If I remember correctly, that conversation concluded that it's not the name, but what's behind the name that's important."

He looked directly at me, held my gaze with those always scanning blue eyes of his. He was searching me, and like an alien probe he registered whatever it was, he found there. Damn, I sure wish I knew what it was.

In half whispered tones I replied, "Yes, it matters to me."

"Very well then. I am called Esaugetuh. [5] I'm a tinkerer, a collector, an illuminator. As you can see, I'm not much of an innkeeper. With that, he turned around and disappeared behind the curtained doorway just as he had the past two nights.

"Tomorrow, yes tomorrow, I'll follow him," I thought as I returned to my cabin. It was four in the morning. I dropped down on the bed and fell asleep.

Giggles woke me. Getting up I peeked out the single window in my cabin. A naked young girl was running from one of the deserted cabins. She was followed by a naked young man. They might have been eighteen but not any more than that. He caught her, laid her gently down on the grass, mounted her eager body, and meeting her upward thrust. I felt like a voyeur; maybe a bit guilty. Somehow their copulation seemed beautiful to me, a rhythmic dance with the universal. Once he had spent himself they got up and left. I heard the purr of a motor as their car drove away. All was quiet. Then off in the distance, a dog bayed.

"Wonder why I continue to stay here? Guess I hadn't gotten the itch to take up the chase again. Maybe there's another reason. One thing is for sure, there's no pretense here. Maybe that's the attraction to the Old One," I thought.

CHAPTER FOUR
HOLOGRAPHIC BEINGS

If we were to look closely at an individual human being, we would immediately notice that it is a unique hologram unto itself; self-contained, self-generating, and self-knowledgeable.
Dr. Ken Dychtwalkd in <u>The Holographic Paradigm</u>

The usual niceties required when two people met were now dropped. Upon seeing me he automatically put food in front of me and began to talk.

"Man," he said, "changes matter by changing his perceptions of it, which in turn creates new entities—new beings, new personalities."

Maybe that's what he trying to do to me, create a new personality, I thought as I sipped the coffee he had placed in front of me.

"We are gods in this sense, creators of new holographic creatures. And that is not such a big deal if you realize that the human brain stores somewhere in the neighborhood of 280 quintillion bits of information. Such creation always requires a change in perception. That is, that change is a conscious act. And this, my young friend, implies the use of *the will*," Esaugetuh said, refilling my coffee cup.

The words 'new beings' brought back the scene I had witnessed earlier. I wonder if new life was created and if those two kids realized the full import of their act. Esaugetuh's voice brought me back from my moment of remembrance, brought me back to the real world. Real world? Shit, who knows what's real anymore? For all I know he could be a holograph. For that matter so could I. Each of us being manipulated by some external energy source.

"The bottom line," Esaugetuh's voice still seemed a long way off, "the bottom line," he repeated, "is fecundity. The creation of new creatures and these new creatures are really little holograms."

"Aren't holograms all the same?" I heard myself saying, somewhat detached.

"No, they can be different gestalts. Remember the story of the *Emperor's New Clothes*?" Esaugetuh asked.

"Vaguely. What about it?"

"Well, the Emperor is the emperor. And that which is created is the creator's hallmark—fecundity."

"If I remember correctly, wasn't the Emperor's new clothes an illusion? He was bare butt naked. I don't get the connection you're trying to make." I said.

"The whole story is an extended metaphor. The Emperor is the illusionary brotherhood of man, that is, that brotherhood which appears not to change. And like the Emperor, it too stands 'bare butt naked' as you put it, before eternity."

"Okay, so the brotherhood of mankind stands, but what about the individual? Is the individual the same over time or is that an illusion?" I asked.

"Adam, if we don't shed the external mask, we appear to be the same over time. Shed the mask, which is Maya, the thing that keeps us from seeing the true nature of the self, we find all of our other selves are illusionary. Little holographs. Let me go back to the Ancient Greeks for a moment."

He paused, brought out the pipe, tapped it on the side of the counter, and took his time to fill it. This seemed to be a habit with him as he searched for the right words or for the next thought he wanted to express. Whatever it was, the aroma helped to cover up the musty smell that enveloped the whole place. Even the food he cooked didn't cover the dank smell for long. It was a welcome relief. Maybe that's why he did it.

"The Ancient Greeks talked of hypocrites. The etymology of that word gives us a clue to my intent here. *Hypo* means under and *krnesthai* to feign to be what one is not—acting. Acting in the Greek tradition involved the use of masks. One's created images are his masks, masks of hypocrisy. We cannot know one another because of these layers of masks, the hypocrisies of our thought patterns. Like these Greek theatre masks, we're an illusion. We don't know the true Self because we haven't removed the masks to all transience. Because we are acting, we have an illusion. Clothed in imaginary clothes. But here's the kicker, this is the reason we are judgmental of one another."

"Judgmental? Aren't we always judgmental and is that not one of the reasons why we wonder who we are over time? Even the child in *The Emperor's*

New Clothes made a judgment when it announced the nakedness of the emperor." I said.

"Ah!" Esaugetuh said, leaning forward, "The child. The child merely told the truth. And in this case, reinforces an important point you must understand."

He was actually glowing, beaming. Pleased with himself, he continued, "You see the child is open to transcendence and as such, provides us with a glimpse of the real Self when it sees the nakedness of the emperor."

"Good god! Are you suggesting that ultimate reality is like the emperor's clothes—an illusion, a holograph, and that it can only be penetrated through transcendence? And are you saying that in the long run, human beings are similar to that illusional realty?" I said.

Such an idea flooded me like an orgasm. I felt the heat on my cheeks as they flushed. It was a tremendous rush and all I could say was "Whew!"

He held his pipe to his lips, waited a moment, and then took a long drag. Ever so slowly he exhaled. Quiet, pensive, lost in thought. And while he was, I looked at him, more closely this time. I swear his hair didn't seem quite so white, that he actually was much younger than I had first imagined. It's an illusion. He's creating that to make a point. On the other hand, I wasn't sure. Maybe it was just the light in the room. It wasn't much to brag about.

Coming from behind the counter Esaugetuh said, "If one arrives at a status or station in life where he may practice the Golden Rule, then that individual remains the same over time. He has no need to be judgmental. The child transcended the illusion and saw the truth and revealed it as such. It made no judgments. Its pronouncement is no different than had it said two plus two are four."

"How does one arrive at this status, this station as you call it, that allows the practice of the Golden Rule?" I asked.

As he sat down on a stool next to me Esaugetuh replied, "Remove Maya— the illusionary world. In doing so you become open to transcendence. The true Self emerges. In the West, such knowledge is equal to cognitive Nirvana."

"I've heard of Nirvana but not cognitive Nirvana. What's that?"

"Oh, it's just my way of saying that Westerners have a different view of enlightenment than do their Eastern counterparts. For them it's a psychological perception that results in some kind of learning," Esaugetuh said.

"And how do I recognize this cognitive Nirvana?" I asked.

"Joe Campbell, the world mythologist, said it better than anybody I know. He said, 'simply follow your bliss,'"

"And that means?"

"To follow what is in your heart or if you prefer, your heart's desire," Esaugetuh said.

"Okay. You said we have shed the mask of illusion, get rid of Maya. How do we do that?"

"By following your bliss!"

"Define bliss," I said.

"It is that which gives you happiness, contentment, and joy in your soul. In psychological terms its Maslow's aesthetic pleasures as stated in his list of hierarchical needs. It's total being. It's Selfhood. It's the very essence of fecundity."

"But my heart's desire may change from day to day, even moment to moment. And man, I'm a damn good example of that. Certainly following my bliss involves risk. Outcomes aren't known."

"That's the essential journey, the magnificent adventure, the ultimate quest! It's Élan, efficacy. Of course, it's a gamble, but what a gamble! Your William Shakespeare summed it up when he wrote, 'The question is to be or not to be.'"

He suddenly got up from the counter stool, exited through the blue curtained doorway, and returned with a bottle and two glasses. He poured two-fingers into each glass.

"Forgot my manners. Ananda, [6]" Esaugetuh said, holding up his glass in salute.

We sat quietly, sipping that wonderfully aged brandy he had given me before. He smoked his pipe and the room was filled with its sweet smelling aroma. It was a nice time; the kind of time I had always thought was the way it should be between a man and his son. Just being together. Words weren't necessary. I broke the silence.

"So how do I come to this Selfhood?"

I wasn't sure at what exact point I had removed the third person from my questions and related them directly to me on a personal level but there it was. He looked at me, his blue eyes a blaze. It seemed an eternity before he answered.

"There are five essential attributes of Selfhood. The first is *mindfulness*. It requires a change in perspective. You have to be aware or *mindful* of all existence. Not just your own. Being mindful of all existence means you respect that existence, paying homage to the rights of all living things. Look at all existence as an act of creative beauty. Have genuine reverence for the very food you eat and those acts necessary for you to nourish yourself. It's much more than the Golden Rule. It's being totally aware of your existence and of extant entities."

"My god!" was all I was able to manage to get out.

"It's something you have yet to learn. Oh, I know you think you are aware but because you are not yet mindful, you are not really aware. It will come when you are centered and are ONE with the world in which you live. The flow of sensory data takes on a whole new and magnificent emotional color and melody as memory's episodic experiences are entered into long-term accounts. Time ceases. There is just now! Of course, you aren't there yet because you haven't changed your perceptions or your perspective. A change in your attitude is absolutely essential. And that, my young friend, is the first step."

"Well old man, I can say this about you. You sure are judgmental," I said gulping the last of the brandy.

Ignoring my comment Esaugetuh said, "There's an old story about a Japanese Master who had a visit from a distinguished professor who had come to inquire about Zen Buddhism. The master, as was his custom, served tea. He poured his visitor's cup full and then continued pouring. The professor, in disbelief, watched this overflow until he couldn't stand it any longer. Blurting out he said, 'Stop! It's overflowing. No more will go in.' The Master replied, 'Like this cup, you are full of your own opinions and speculations. How can I show you Zen unless you first empty your cup?'" [7]

"Okay. I've been told. I get it," I said, "But how do I empty my cup so I may become mindful?"

"Get rid of your preconceived ideas, notions, and beliefs. The Frenchman, Descartes, said it, 'Reject everything until you no longer can doubt it.'"

With that said, Esaugetuh relit his pipe, got up from his stool, and went out through the blue-curtained doorway. I remembered I had vowed to follow him. I hurried through the doorway. There was nothing there. No room, no Esaugetuh. Just open space.

"You cannot see beyond the parted curtain because you are not ready."

His voice came from nowhere but at the same time, it came from everywhere. The hair on my arms stood up. I sensed a strong electrical impulse and the smell of ozone burned my nostrils. I turned and ran back through the blue-curtained doorway expecting at any moment to be struck by a bolt of lightning.

CHAPTER FIVE
THE GOD QUALITY

Man-the-less must become Man-the-more and that man is deity-in-posse.
Troy Wilson Organ
(The Hindu Quest for the Perfection of Man)

I cannot remember a time when my parents walked off and left a guest, even during those halcyon days with the Indians in Quebec Province. Sometimes then, a couple of the Indian women would come to our small cabin to visit. During that time I was expected to follow the rule of 'being seen but not heard.' The ladies of the teepees would stay most of the day, smoke a pipe, and have two glasses of whiskey. They did very little talking. I felt Esaugetuh 's sudden departures were rude, especially since he didn't even excuse himself. So I decided to confront him about his disappearing act. If he didn't want my company all he had to do was not invite me to stay after my meal. The bottom line is I don't have to stay here.

"Why do you insist on denying that which is?" Esaugetuh replied to my confrontation.

"Now what the hell are you talking about? I suppose you're going to tell me I have been hallucinating? Shit, I might even be hallucinating—right now—right here," I snapped.

I was so angry I was shaking. I lost all control. "My god," I thought, "Maybe I'm hallucinating?

Maybe I'm caught in some time warp or weird virtual reality thing?"

The sweet smell of his tobacco reaching out from the reality I so wanted, assured me I wasn't. And of course, I knew why I stayed.

"Adam, the entire physical universe itself is nothing more than patterns of neuronal energy firing off inside of your head and everyone else's, for that matter," Esaugetuh said calling me by my name for only the second time. "Say, are you all right?"

"What? Yeah. I'm just fine. How the hell do you think I am?"

"Okay, if you say so, but perhaps a brandy?" Esaugetuh said.

"No! I said I was fine. Damn it. Leave it at that."

Ignoring me, he shoved a snifter of the aged brandy across the counter to me. Its sweet nutty smell tantalized my nose. Instead of gulping it down I took a small amount in my mouth, rolled it around on my tongue, savoring its flavor. I don't know what brand it was, but it was exceptional. So smooth. I waited for him to begin.

"We operate as cognitional multidimensional projections. These holograms are the catalysts for our thought processes. Even though they essentially remain unchanged, they enter into and facilitate our thought processes. They render reality," Esaugetuh said. "The Greeks understood this. They created their gods in their own images and they did this because they realized that the invisible, that which cannot be named, had to be understood by the visible. The visible being man."

"What in the hell do you mean by 'cognitional multidimensional projections'?"

"Thought projections on many levels or dimensions. All exists as projection. But right now, I want to come back to the Greeks. Making the invisible visible is truly their greatest miracle. That allowed them to humanize the world and that freed all future civilizations from the paralyzing fear of an omnipotent unknown. Zeus was a known with human traits and foibles. They could live with that.

Today's world, modern civilization, modern man no longer knows the truth. The center is unknown to them. Reality does not exist. It's a celluloid world. It's a flash, momentary and brings only momentary gratification. Unfortunately, the modern world is composed of instant oatmeal, instant potatoes, instant soups, and instant whole meals. Instant relationships and instant lives. Nothing else exists."

"You're agreeing that Nietzsche was right when he said, 'God is dead' even though polls show that 85% of Americans believe there is a god?"

"Their belief in a living viable god is questionable. I'm afraid for many it's illusionary," Esaugetuh replied, smoke billowing up from his pipe.

Continuing he said, "In the ancient literature of India there is a prayer that is a good mantra.
From the unreal lead me to the real!
From the darkness lead me to the light!
From death lead me to immortality! [8]

"Nice," I said.

"It's a petition," Esaugetuh replied.

"A petition?"

"Yes. It's a petition to allow the individual to be lead away from the world of illusion to reality; to be lead away from ignorance to knowledge, and to be lead away from death to immortality."

"There's an implied progression, isn't there?"

"Yes. Hopefully to a higher level. Man is capable of tremendous expansion. He is capable of moving from his ignorance and present concept of reality to a new consciousness. Once he does that, he is free of being time-bounded. He becomes deity-in-posse!"

"Deity in what? Man, are you sure you're not on some loco weed?" I said.

The smoke rings really took off. I'd not noticed their size before. When he was pleased they grew larger, all encompassing. When he was displeased the rings narrowed, and when he was really pissed, the rings shot up like steam from an old coal-fired locomotive straining with a heavy load. Maybe that's the way he felt about me. Maybe I was a heavy load when it came to understanding.

"the potentiality. . ."

"of man being god. Talk about reality. I think you're the one who better get real, old man."

There I was attacking again. Wonder if that's why my old man and I didn't get along. Oh, we didn't have fights, nothing ever physical. Not even screaming matches but there was always a sharpness there.

"Why should that shock you? That idea is as old as is man himself. In the literature of Ancient

Greece, we find evidence of such a notion and they were supposed to be highly civilized. The Titans killed the son of Zeus. In retaliation Zeus destroyed them. Out of their ashes, man rose up and because the Titans had eaten the flesh of Dionysus, a god, that spark of divinity was passed to man. That's one basis for acknowledging the divinity of man. In Christianity, you are told that God created man in his own image."

Esaugetuh's words barely had been given breath when there was a loud clap of thunder. It shook the office-café. A rush of wind came through the open window clearing the room of his tobacco smoke. In that moment of distraction, he was gone!

Not a sign of him anywhere. I poked my head through the blue-curtained doorway. Nothing just as before. Empty space.

I went back to my cabin more perplexed than ever. To say that man is potentially God is—is just too damn much! The old man was getting to me and I didn't like it one damn bit. Just who in the hell does he think he is anyway, God?

CHAPTER SIX
THE GOD QUALITY CONTINUED

Possunt Quia Posse Videntur (They can because they think they can)
Vergil (The Aeneid 5:231)

It was an ungodly hour when I was awakened by a knock on my cabin door. I fumbled around for the light, struggled to see the time as I squinted at my watch. Jesus, 3:30. The knock turned into a loud banging.

"Just a damn minute," I yelled.

I looked out the one window and could see no one. Thinking that it might be the three people in the truck at the gas station, I pulled out my Glock automatic from my backpack. As I shoved the clip home and slammed a shell into the chamber I grabbed my flashlight.

"Who's there and what do you want?"

"It's Esaugetuh. May we talk?"

I unlocked the door, opened it just a crack and turned on the flashlight to make sure it was him. Then I let him in.

"You always pack an automatic?" Esaugetuh said.

"You always wake people up at 3:30 in the morning?"

"I do when it's important. I need to clarify a few points. Don't want you to misunderstand."

"Misunderstand what?" I said, indicating that he should sit down in the one chair in the cabin.

As Esaugetuh sat down he pulled out the now ever present pipe, tapped it on a rung of the chair, filled it, lit it, and took a long slow drag, filling his lungs. He exhaled even slower. The smell was a welcome reprieve from the musty dank smell of the cabin.

"I wasn't saying that man could become God or any other name you may attach to that which is, that which always has been, that which is all pervasive. In Chinese it's Tao. It has been called Yahweh, Allah, The Logos, Nature, The Absolute, Élan Vital, The Oversoul, Heavenly Father, and then there's Freud's Cosmic Libido. By whatever name you choose, in the human being, it is the Self. It is that which exists, that which is all controlling. And it is that that is deity in posse. I want to talk about that."

After that Esaugetuh took another draw on his pipe. Noticing that I enjoyed its rich aroma Esaugetuh pulled a small dish out of his pocket, sat it down on the nightstand, and then put a pinch of his tobacco in it.

"You got matches?"

"No," I replied puzzled by his actions.

"Here. Always carry at least three matches with you. Light the tobacco when you want. It'll refresh the room. Help you sleep. If you like it, I'll give you some more later."

"Ah, a peace offering," I thought.

"The Sanskrit word *Deva* meant divinity. And like a lot of things it's undergone several changes. Today it implies energy, a special energy, and divine in nature. It has come to mean richness in potentialities," Esaugetuh said.

"So."

"Man is the repository of this special energy. Some folks probably would call this spiritual energy." He stopped, looked at me, and then continued, "We went through this naming business earlier so I hope you're not going to start that all over again," Esaugetuh said.

"No argument from me."

"Good. As a receptor for this divine energy, man has tremendous potentiality. He has god-like potential. Once he learns to unlock this potential there's the chance of it being used for good or evil. Evil is probably not quite the right choice of words here. More likely it would be blundering stupidity. Many are concerned about that. And rightly so. Animals have been cloned; life in a Petri dish has been created, embryonic and stem cell research opens the portal to life everlasting—maybe. There needs to be a concern as to how deity in posse affects man in his interpersonal relationship, his relationship to the natural world, and his relationship to the cosmos itself."

"This relationship business really bothers you, doesn't it?" I said.

"Yes. And it should you. Man is the key to cosmic process. In him, reality is most fully manifest for he is the ultimate Self-aware being. If he becomes aware only of himself, that is, in ego building, any potential for a unique role within the cosmic structure is negated. I'm concerned because *posse* has a double meaning: To be able to have power. And it is been interpreted to mean power over others, as power over nature rather than power within. It's the power within that is the miracle maker. The potential is there. And now I have a question to leave you with. What is your potential?"

"Do you mean my potential to be a successful writer, research analyst?"

"In the *Chandogya Upanishad,* it says, 'Man is the Self, yet he must become the Self. Until he knows who he is, he is less than he is.' Get some rest. We'll talk again later," Esaugetuh, said, getting up to leave. "I'll shut the door behind me."

CHAPTER SEVEN
THE SERPENT IN THE GARDEN

When there's a transformation in your own consciousness, there is a proportional and corresponding transformation in the world, in the reality of your experience.
Tau Malachi
(The Gnostic Gospel of St. Thomas)

The Florida sunrise was spectacular. Its golden orange hues stretched outward and upward, hand-like with its fingers forcing the night shadows back to the other side of the world. A mourning dove cooed as a cardinal flitted from tree to tree. The day was going to be hot, too hot to stay cooped up in a small cabin.

Besides, there wasn't a chance in hell that I could sleep after Esaugetuh's latest revelation. He's either one of the world's most brilliant or a crazy old man who has been alone far too long. Having decided to go for a walk, I left my cabin.

Walking along a meandering path, weed-grown with clumps of wild flowers plopped down here and there—gifts from the birds—I came upon a small lake, actually a pond, sequestered among the palmettos and scrub pines. It glistened in the early sunlight, made diamond-like by a sea fog that still remained. An egret, flapping its wings in preparation for flight, broke the quietness of the place. The musty mildew smell of the cabin was replaced by honeysuckle and jasmine vine.

Stretching out on the narrow shore of the pond, I gazed up at the morning sky so perfectly framed by the palmettos and pine. A painter's dream, peaceful, serene. The sun warmed me. I dozed off wondering what my potentialities were.

A rustling sound woke me. As I lifted my head I looked into the open mouth of a rattlesnake curled upon my chest. Its tongue flicked in and out and my heart went into overdrive so fast that I thought I was passing out. Frozen with fear, my life flashed before me. Suddenly everything went black. The sun had disappeared. I was sure I had been bitten and was dying of heart failure. I couldn't even moan.

"When you're out in the scrub, you best keep an eye open for snakes," Esaugetuh said as he released the snake from his grip so it could go about its business.

"Whew! I sure thought I was a goner. I owe you!" I said, looking up at him. His eyes seemed bluer than the morning sky.

Our gaze locked for a nanosecond and in that very brief moment, I understood nothing more had to be said. It was a closed incident. He extended his hand to help me up. I was still shaken.

"There is a consciousness, a human consciousness connected to the cosmos, that exists," Esaugetuh said as he gazed out over the pond. "It's pregnant with unrealized values," he paused and then continued, "values, mind you, that transcend because man himself is transcendent. Because of this transcendence man discovers those values which conjoin with his inherent potentialities. It is a universal, a given, that man seeks value."

"I remember something about transcendence from philosophy classes at the University. Kant was into all that. So what's new about what you just said?"

Replying, Esaugetuh said, "It is the search! It's the quest for and the understanding of those universals that enables man. It is the questing, the activity of questing, through which the very essence of man is revealed. It's what activates him."

Okay, so man is restless! He's always been a mover. History books are filled with the stories of brave men and women who have gone on quests. Big deal!"

"Your question should be 'why'," Esaugetuh, snorted.

"The answer is simple. Man is never satisfied. He's never satisfied because nothing brings him permanent satisfaction," I said, feeling irritated.

"You've missed the point. The very fact that man is dissatisfied with his finite nature shows that it is not his natural condition."

"So—?"

The question-answer period was annoying me and it seemed to be annoying me more than usual. It had set my teeth on edge. I didn't understand his grilling me about my beliefs, my thoughts, and feelings.

Unruffled by my coolness Esaugetuh said, "Man has an insatiable hunger. The fact that it's insatiable is just one small demonstration that man by his very nature is infinite, and one reason that he's deity in posse."

"Look, I've had it. I've been up half the damn night. A rattler nearly got me and you're telling me I'm infinite because of insatiable hunger. And all of that is based on the assumption that I give a rat's ass."

I spun around and headed back to my cabin. Hurrying along the path I had taken earlier, I remembered to look where I was stepping. All I needed was another close encounter with a rattler. Once I reached my cabin, I flopped down on the lumpy bed. Its mildew smell seemed worse than ever. Because there wasn't a screen on the window I didn't open it. I didn't need a hoard of flying insects in here. And I didn't want to leave the door open and unlocked. I rolled over, nearly knocking the little nightstand over. The dish with the tobacco in it came into my view. I sat up, lit one of the three matches Esaugetuh gave me and lit the tobacco. I gently blew on it to make sure it was burning. Then I lay back down.

My mind was engaged in an endless shouting match. What are my potentialities? Why am I so angry at this old man? He's not forcing me to stay here. Maybe I should get out. No, I really don't want to leave. The voices slammed against one another. My head throbbed. I didn't know which voice to listen to. There is just so much confusion. "Jesus, I'm losing it," I said out loud. The sound of my voice brought me back to reality. Reality? Hell, what's that? How do I know who I am anyway? For that matter, how does anyone know who they are?

Questions! Questions! They never seem to stop. Maybe I really should move on. Maybe I should turn around and go back to New York, marry Jacqueline, have two and a quarter kids, statistically speaking. At least the tobacco was making the place smell a bit better. I rolled over, buried my head under my pillow, and tried to go to sleep.

CHAPTER EIGHT
MIRROR, MIRROR

In appearance, I'm a thing moving about in space.
In reality, I'm that unmoving space itself.
Douglas Harding

The shouting match in my head exhausted me but not so tired that certain biological urges couldn't make themselves known. The teen-agers getting it on flashed into memory.

"Lucky son-of-a-bitch."

"So who am I? How does anyone know who they are? How did it go? 'Mirror, mirror on the wall.' Instead of asking who's the fairest of all, I guess I should ask who's the dumbest of all.

"You are!" was my resounding answer.

"And so I am!" I said.

A quick shower and shave made me feel better. I thought the water had a sulfur smell about it, but what the hell, what can you expect out in the Green Swamp? As I strolled into the café the smell of freshly brewed coffee wafted between ham and eggs greeted me. Not only was I hungry for sex, but also for food. Both issues had not gone unnoticed by my friend. "My friend? I'll be—,"

"Well," Esaugetuh smirked, "Young fella, looks like you need a night in town. It's Saturday night and we don't provide certain services here."

"But—I—how—,"

"How? Good lord, don't tell me you expect me to teach you that, too? Guess you are dumber than I first thought," Esaugetuh roared with raucous laughter.

"Okay, knock it off. What I was trying to see was how do you know what I need?"

"Knowing you need sex is easy. You're showing yourself. Go on, go into town. I'm sure there're some women available at the bar. You won't be worth a tinker's damn as long as you're in heat. We'll talk when you get back," Esaugetuh said.

His eyes had a mischievous twinkle in them. A wide circle of pipe smoke floated about his hoary head, halo-like.

"That old fart is enjoying all of this—the idea of me getting laid. What the hell, why not?" I thought.

The drive into town was uneventful. The flatbed truck was parked in a field and the men who had been in it while I was buying gas looked up from their work and waved. I honked the horn and sped on by. At mid-day there weren't many people in the bar. One woman, not my type, was messing around with two older men in one of the darker corners. I had decided that the whole thing was a bad idea when a young woman came in through a side door.

She had long dark hair, large doe-eyes, and full lips. She was probably twenty something. Without hesitating, she came up to me at the bar, slid up on one of the stools next to me.

"Buy me a drink?"

It was late when I got back to the motel. Esaugetuh was waiting for me.

"Well, you feeling better?"

"Yeah," I said dryly.

Actually, I wasn't feeling a whole lot better. The woman was like a mechanical robot. No feeling, no personality. No warmth. She just laid there and let me pump away as she chewed her gum. There was no sense of being and because she was that way, I felt my being was denied. My being? Who in the hell is the *I* of me anyway? This body over which I claim ownership? My self? My soul?"

Esaugetuh looked at me with those penetrating blue eyes of his. He knew I didn't really have a great time. He sensed my very personal embarrassment and disgust.

"Adam you're struggling with an age old dilemma. The true *I-am* needs no support, no grounding. For heaven's sake, boy, who would be able to substantiate it? It is the ground itself—the ground of all other grounding, all proof. For consciousness, being must first exist. For awareness of being, consciousness of Self must exist—the I-*am* must be recognized.

"So I must recognize the 'I' of my being?" I said.

"Yes. That's a beginning. Human beings act and think, consciously expressed publicly or in personal silence. Whichever it is, they cry out, 'we are body, soul, self, sensation, action, and thinking. We are alive!' But when a person calls himself these things, that person lives a contradiction," Esaugetuh said.

"A contradiction?"

"Yes. It's a contradiction because '**I**' can only be *I*, not the one who feels himself to be all this, but the one who knows, thinks, and ultimately brings utterance to all assertions. I cannot point to anything outside of myself, spirit, body, or soul and still that I am that. I can only be the one who says this. Thus **I** express a contradiction. All that I hold in this way as my being are merely things, manifestations, so to speak. I look in a mirror, look at myself, see the image, and say to myself, 'I am that.' And that's what you've been trying to do."

"Looking in a mirror and seeing myself doesn't tell me who I am?"

"Correct. You are still doing that and that's the problem. You are still trying to identify yourself with the mirrored image. It is not an illuminated image and as such, it is impossible for you to realize that *you* are not that image in the mirror. You are the one who sees it, the one who knows himself in that mirror. It is this mirrored image that places you in the contradiction by not recognizing that it is the *I-of-you* who places, who speaks, who thinks, who dreams, and who is the final causation of all that you are or ever hope to be."

"But don't we, I mean, don't I carry this mirror with me?"

"Always. The mirror, four cornered as Sylvia Plath would have you believe or round, or oval, it is always present. But Adam shouldn't your question be what is the mirror?"

The pipe smoke was billowing. I wasn't even aware that he had lit it. It had become so much of our nightly conversations that I no longer brought it to consciousness.

"The mirror that you always carry with you, that inner eye, is your Self, and in that mirror is the 'I' that you perceive. It is the personal, individual, autobiographical Self. Human beings are body and Self and are recognized by their inner 'I' as such. As long as they live with this, without struggle, they may live with the agonizing contradiction. The problem comes about when human beings attempt to conceptualize and express this. The paradox is born and manifests itself in what is experienced as the eternal quest for the ultimate."

"Okay. I'm body and Self, but what is wrong with looking for what you call the ultimate?"

"Ah! But what is your ultimate?" Esaugetuh said, eyes narrowing as he searched me for what I would say."

"Truth!"

"Truth? You seek the truth! Nonsense! Seeking the truth is not the issue. The issue is recognition. Can you, or anyone else for that matter, recognize the truth when you see it? Have you recognized the truth of your own being? I think not! You still view yourself as body-mind. You went into town, got laid, had your biological need met. That's body-mind thinking; Self recognition."

"So what the hell's wrong with my getting laid? Shit! Don't tell me you never have any 'body needs'?"

"My body needs are not the issue here. Don't try to redirect the conversation away from the issue. The issue is whether or not you can handle the ultimate truth. Let's put it to a test. You are not and cannot be body. Unfortunately for some, the realization that they, in all truth, cannot just be body-mind causes them to have a split-mind as Alan Watts called it."

"How in hell can that be?" I grumbled.

"It's because it's not the body that speaks, thinks, nor does it say, 'I am.' Descartes' 'I think therefore I exist' and the Existentialist pronouncement, 'I exist; therefore I am!' provides a clue," Esaugetuh said.

"How's that?"

"The expression of the personal pronoun reveals it is the Self, not the body which is the initiator of all action. It is the Self, the *I* who thinks identity. It's not that *I* in the mirror image, but that which sees it. Remember this above all else, your I is the center. It cannot be demonstrated. It's invisible. It has not been seen. It will not be seen. It's nothing that can ever be seen. Why? Because it is ITSELF seeing, processing, knowing it. It's existence!"

Silence. Absolute silence surrounded us as we sat there, timeless and speechless with all eternity passing between us. The unmistakable rustle of a snake gliding across the old wooden floor broke that silence and I felt death pass within inches of my legs. Esaugetuh, not at all bothered, bent down as the Pygmy rattler lifted its head, flicked its tongue seeking identification. Satisfied, the snake slithered its way on to Esaugetuh's outstretched hand. It coiled, reared its flat head back as if it was about to strike. My heart was racing so fast I was sure I was going into hyperventilation. It didn't strike.

"Thank you," Esaugetuh said. "I'll tend to it." With that said, he gently placed the small snake on the floor of the café. Then he looked at me; a half smile spread across his face, bemused.

Then looking directly at me with those azure blue eyes of his he said, "The notion that human beings perceive only phenomena for which they have pre-conceptualizations or ideas is untenable and is especially so when applied to the observation of consciousness. Such a notion denies the workings of the Self. For example, what is it you've just observed?"

"A god damned rattler curled upon your hand. You must be insane1"

"But was it real or illusion? Did you see it with your Self or with your body-mind? Which mirrored image is the *I* going to accept is dependent upon your understanding of what I have been telling you—here, now!"

"I—,"

"You need to move your car from in front of your cabin. And move your gear to cabin seven. You are to spend the night there. Bad storm coming. The roof on four is not the best of shape."

"What? How do you know that?" I stammered.

"Good night," Esaugetuh said, leaving through the blue curtained doorway. He suddenly stopped, turned and said, "I'm serious, Adam; don't go back to your old cabin. Do you understand? You are not to spend the night there. Get your stuff and car out of there and do it now! Do exactly as I tell you."

His tenseness as he left the room unnerved me. A flash crossed the darkening sky. Lightening! Sharp and piercing. Ozone filled the room. I ran to my cabin, stuffed my stuff into my backpack, jumped into my car, and moved it to cabin seven. The rain had begun by the time I got into number seven. I barely got the door bolted when there was the loudest clap of thunder I had ever heard in my life. It was deafening. Then came rapid non-stop lightening. Volley after volley slashed through the night. It danced around my cabin. Neons of red, red-orange and blue-green blistering white flashes cut grotesque shapes on the walls of my cabin. It was shaking so fiercely that the one window shattered and glass flew everywhere. The door blew open and I was knocked to my knees. Terrified, I slithered, snake-like, across the wooden floor, desperate for safety. There was none. I curled into a ball and lay there.

"My god! The end has come." I moaned.

CHAPTER NINE
MIRROR, MIRROR CONTINUED

We human beings consider ourselves to be made up of "sold matter." Actually, the physical body is the end product, so to speak, of the subtle information fields, which mold our physical body as well as all physical matter.
Itzhak Bentov
Stalking the Wild Pendulum

As I crawled out from beneath my overturned bed the last thing I remembered from the previous violence was one gigantic thunderclap. Cautiously I looked out the opening that once had a door. I clutched onto the door casing to steady myself. My head was spinning; the whole place was spinning. I felt I was caught up in a vortex. Whatever I had felt as being solid was being challenged as all turned into oscillating waves. You've seen those come up off the hood of a car that been in the sun or that has been driven for a long period of time.

With what I felt as a Herculean effort I got out onto the small porch. There wasn't a whole lot of it left. I tried to steady myself and not touch any part of the porch structure for fear it would collapse on me. Lots of debris were strewn around. Small stuff, mostly. Birds were everywhere, flitting around, and screeching. Some kind of a rodent, probably a possum scurried from under the porch. I looked back up the row of cabins. Number four was a pile of rubble. I mean it was flattened. A chill washed over me. I shuddered.

"We experience certain elements of consciousness, thoughts, and concepts, without having the sensation of reality. Isn't that what all of this is about? Sensations! Jesus! I'm sure having plenty of them right now," I said out loud.

The yellowish hue of the place, sky, trees, grass, and plants didn't help me feel things were still real. I was sure I had been transported into a Dali painting of a surrealistic nightmare in which everything is dissected into garish distortions. Or maybe I was time-warped into an Edgar Allan Poe horror story. Whatever the hell it was that had just happened it took me back to one summer on the lake in Canada. A sudden storm had come up on the lake and our small boat was tossed about like a piece of straw. Somehow my father managed to beach the boat. Sand peppered us, cutting deep into my skin, stinging like thousands of angry bees. I was sure we would be marooned there and die.

Wonder where Esaugetuh is? Sure hope the old fart is okay. Man, he's something else.

"Coffee? Straight or laced?"

There he was. Just like that. Out of nowhere in particular; yet from everywhere. As I stepped off the unstable porch I said, "Straight."

"Come along, then."

At the café he poured us both coffee as he said, "Yours is laced. You look like death warmed over. You okay?" Esaugetuh said.

He waited for me to take my first sip. It was good. The brandy set it up. Putting his cup down, he took out his clay pipe, filled it, and lit it. Between the brandied coffee and the smell of the Kinnikinnick tobacco an aura of comfort flowed over me. If wasn't until my cup was half empty did he speak.

"So you're still wondering about consciousness and reality are you?"

"Man, after last night's hell on earth, I'm not sure what reality is. Half the time I'm not sure if I'm even conscious. Yet, I know that we are supposed to accept our thoughts and concepts as being real. We have them; therefore, they exist. I experience them; you experience them. At least for a nanosecond. If that's true, then I don't see the need for a 'sensation' of reality—of being conscious. Sensation only suggests and any given sensation I may have at any moment may be illusionary. Sure hope last night was illusionary. What the hell happened? How'd you know I should move out of cabin four?" I said.

"Last night was very real. The snake told me. When you live out here as long as I have you learn to listen to nature's warnings. Enough about that."

"Isn't it obvious that 'sensed reality' doesn't appear real because of its conceptual nature? Don't we need a feeling of evidence, that is, something solid to experience reality? Isn't that what we do? Don't we concretize everything, even down to a nanosecond?" I asked.

"Adam, your still dissecting—cutting everything up into little bits and pieces. When you continually break everything down into its constituent parts you miss that which is. What you need to do is to get a synoptic view. When you have that, your consciousness will recognize its truth and reality will be born. Percept and concept have to be united if there is to be wholeness. Unfortunately many people remain separated from that possible unification and struggle all of their lives as split minds, miserable and desperate. They are to be pitied. Like the people in Plato's *Allegory of the Cave*, they may destroy those who have become unified into a total synthesis of truth, sensation, and reality, that is, those who have become a Self."

"Hmm. So what you're talking about is total synthesis? Is such a thing really possible? I said.

"It's possible! No, not people like Einstein, Nietzsche, or Goethe. Actually they were quite closed-minded. Einstein got hung up on his unification principle, Nietzsche his Greek tragedy, and Goethe had his narrowness of insight. Oh, I know, literary and scientific types make a great deal of them. Take Newton, for example, what did he actually achieve after his *Principa?* If not these people, who then? Buddha? Zarathustra? Mohammed? Christ? Maybe Mother Teresa or the late Pope John Paul, II?"

"Is it possible for one to receive both concept and percept simultaneously and not as separate entities?" I asked.

"Yes it's possible. Such a mind would never consider the two as separate but would render both concept and percept to be indivisible and inexorably bound with its object. So, where does that leave the ***I-Am,*** the Self?"

"Well—, it seems to me, that what you're saying is that the ***I's*** experience of itself creates the ***I*** without knowledge of itself. An ***I*** without being cannot be reality."

"No! A thousand times no! My god, you sure haven't learned much. Don't you really listen?" Esaugetuh blurted as smoke rings zoomed out of his pipe and collided with one another as they raced for the top of the ceiling.

"Go back to the mirror." Esaugetuh continued, "Go to the image. Was it not the ***I*** who placed 'you' in front of the mirror? Was that you, the ***I***? No! The ***I*** was the initiator of the action. It cannot be seen."

"But," I protested.

"Granted," Esaugetuh continued, "there is a self-sensing and with this self-sensing comes the development of the subconscious. The ego is thus reflected self-sensing—a self-sensing reflection of the ***I.*** It's self-sensing; not self-aware and that's the reason for the search, isn't it?"

"So you're saying our perceptual world is metamorphosed and we become convinced that our percepts exist, that they are real? That the ***I of me*** is real?"

"The only way for an ***I*** to live is to live in identity. It's the ***I*** that guides, moves, and initiates. As you become aware of your attention as a creative reality, that reality lifts you up to the most intimate and individual activity of the ***I***. When the ***I-experience*** occurs in a perceptible attention, it's climactic, not unlike the orgasm you should have experienced with the young woman in town. The total being is bathed in an exquisite sensational rush that explodes upon the *I* bringing it to a new level of consciousness. At that point, *deity in posse* exists. It is the creation of the Self. You, yourself, are the solution to the riddle of nature because you have it within you, at least the potentiality and that potentiality is *deity in posse*. Creation personified. And that is fecundity!"

"Oh man! How can you compare something like that to that not so great an encounter I had in town? There was no rocket's red glare. Come on, you're sure reaching," I said.

"No, you miss the point. The orgasm you experienced in town was not the way it should have or could have been because you were not functioning in an *I-am* mode but in a body-mind mode. A passage from one of my favorites works, the *Upanishad* [9].

> *He who, dwelling in all things,*
> *Yet is other than all things,*
> *Whom all things do not know*
> *Whose body all things are,*
> *Who controls all things within,*
> *He is your Soul, the Inner*
> *Controller, the Immortal.*

"And that brings me to another attribute of Selfhood. Do you remember the first one?" Esaugetuh asked. He had that twinkle back in his eyes.

"Sure. It's mindfulness," I said, pleased with myself for remembering.

"Maybe there's hope for you yet, young fella. This one gets a bit tricky because it involves the pleasure principle and at the same time encompasses something more. Your lack of real satisfaction in your recent tryst in town is because you realized that something more than mere release had to be involved. You viewed the woman as being of less value than yourself, as a vehicle, mechanical in function and as something existing for your own personal release. A paid object. The something more you missed involves a deep and genuine appreciation for all that exists from that woman to the micro and macrocosmic realities that are existent. It's Maslow's 'ah ha' experience of self-actualization, that Eureka, that Satori of joy as well as cultivating that in all things. Accept each blade of grass as a thing of worth, each grain of sand as a work of art, as things of beauty, each existence as a unique masterpiece. Get involved in that uniqueness and you will find joy in that existence and maybe, just maybe, you might experience a sense of that which is divine in you. Even the lowly worm that crawls upon its belly through the bowels of the earth has its value and worth. This ***joyfulness*** is the ultimate recognition of Selfhood in all living things," Esaugetuh said, tapping his pipe on the counter.

"But,"

"Enough! I'm tired. Leave me to my peace."

With that, he left back through the blue-curtained doorway. I went back to my cabin. I felt tired, weary of all the talk. I wondered why I was still staying here.

I'm supposed to be looking for a shaman. He probably doesn't exist anyway. Shit, I've forgotten all about him. Oh! Man! Am I ever stupid? Esaugetuh! That son-of-a-bitch! And he's known all along I was looking for him. He's been playing games with me. Damn! I've been had and big time.

With that revelation, I felt as if I had been gut-kicked by a mule. As I slumped down into the old chair a quiver ran through my body and I broke out in a cold sweat.

What I jerk I've been. Okay, enough is enough already. It's time for this crap shoot to stop. He's been playing me, a god damn toy for his amusement.

I hurled myself out of the lumpy chair, bolted out the door and ran to the café. My anger was surpassed only by my total surprise when I realized I was staring at an empty room. No grill, no counter, and no coffee pot. Nothing. I was shaking so hard I could hardly stand still. A quick search of the building reinforced the so painfully obvious. It was deserted and had been for a long time. Swirling around, I ran back out the door to see if my car was still there. It was parked in front of the old motel just as I had parked it. A line from Keats popped into my head, "Was it a vision, or a waking dream? Fled is that music:—do I wake or sleep?" [10]

My God! Have I gone over the edge? Totally lost it?

I walked back to cabin seven, a shack, picked up my backpack and sleeping bag and went to my car. As I approached I spotted the three men from the gas station pulling into the motel entrance. I felt uneasy and I had learned long ago to pay heed to those feelings. I reached for my gun, eased the safety off, and walked toward my car.

The driver of the old truck leaned out the window and said, "The man at the gas place said you were staying out here. This is not a good place. Angelina says you should come back into town. Fact is she wants us to help you, make sure you come back."

I noticed the other two had gotten out of the truck. I unlocked my rental, tossed in my gear. Pulled out the Glock automatic, fired one round into the ground.

"Back off! Be quick about it."

The two jumped back on the truck's bed as it sped off.

As I got into the car I stepped on something. It was just lying there. Esaugetuh's clay pipe. I reached down and picked it up. The strange intoxicating smell of the Kinnikinnick lingered. Then I realized it was still warm from being smoked.

"Damn!" I said, revving the motor and the car shot forward.

CHAPTER TEN
AT THE MESA

One common mistake is to think that one reality is the reality. You must always be prepared to leave one reality for a greater one.
Mother Meera

Before I had ended up in Florida I had considered going to Colorado because there was a pow-wow going on there and I had planned on interviewing some of the medicine men. Now, however, if my hunch was correct my elusive shaman would be headed there. As soon as I hit I-4 I used my cell phone to call for a flight to Denver and a connecting flight to Durango. No more tricks. Lady Luck was with me. A seat was available and I could make a connection out of Denver. I barely made Tampa International because of a pile up on the Interstate.

Anyway, here I am headed for Denver, then a shuttle into Durango, and then a trip over winding roads to the mesa. I had called ahead asking for a rental. I hoped they had something decent waiting for me. I had told the agency I needed something with enough room to stow camping gear. I gave them a list of what I wanted and a credit card number.

At nearly thirty thousand feet you certainly do get a different perspective. Looking out the window I could see the ever changing mass of white with its commingling shadows filled with an accretion of unfathomable mysteries, reflected light and dark anatomies, and occasionally pierced with golden arrows emphasized by patch-work azure. I looked down at earth-bound ant patterns crisscrossing, intersecting, and bisecting. Conglomerations of emeralds and topaz.

The steward stopped and asked if I wanted a drink. He brought me a martini with a small package of cashews. The man sitting next to me, middle-age and balding, had already slurped down two doubles. That's all I needed was a drunk for a seat companion. I had just about made up my mind to ask for another seat when he turned to me and spoke for the first time.

"I'm on my way to Denver to go to a funeral."

"Someone close to you?" I heard myself saying. My voice sounded even shallow to me.

"You could say that," He said. "The name's Talbot. George Talbot."

"I'm sorry to hear of your loss," I said, taking the first sip of my martini.

"Not much of a drinker, I see."

"Excuse me?" I said.

"Well, you've had that drink for several minutes and that's the first you've touched it."

"It would have been rude of me to drink it while you were talking to me," I said.

I couldn't believe I had actually said that. I stirred the olive around in the glass, avoiding eye contact with the man next to me.

"Yeah, I'm going to a funeral."

"You said that," I replied.

"Uh huh. I'm going to my own funeral. Ya see I'm the one dying. At first, I thought it was a hell of a thing. I'm just fifty. Thought I had lots of time left. I figured wrong. I have a tumor on my heart. Inoperable. What do you think about that?"

I said nothing, turning to look out the window, and letting my thoughts wander. Sure I know that feelings, thoughts, concepts, and ideas are merely surface activities functioning to sense self—rushing headlong, flooding, washing this self—this same self into its own being. And like the butterfly emerging from its private cocoon, it finally breaks into winged flight of its own being—graceful; yet, strong in its new found freedom of self-recognition. Then—then it realizes the fullness of its own beauty and wonderment, for it exists!

Suddenly I snapped out of myself. It came to me like an unexpected shot. This ultimate truth that man seeks is a smile between God and himself— between one divinity and another—a breaking smile across open lips as they form the boundaries of recognition. And I wanted him to know that especially since I had set up a boundary between us by turning my back to him.

I heard myself saying, "You are that, that you are."

"What?"

"You are what you are, my friend, and those who have judged your life may be wrong."

"Sure would be nice if what you said turned out to be true."

"And when you find you still have time left, what will you do with that time?" I asked.

"Live, of course, wouldn't you?"

And I would, I thought.

But what I wanted to ask him was how he would live differently if he found he wasn't about to die, but the pilot's announcement of our beginning descent to Denver's airport interrupted.

George Talbot got off the plane ahead of me. Before I could disembark, a member of the crew had to hand carry my revolver off the plane. It was in a locked case. Ammunition was in my luggage. It bothered me that I had not said more to Talbot. I wasn't sure if I had been mindful enough. I decided that if I had to ask myself that kind of question, I had not been. I should have told him there was still time for him to find joy, time to bring joy to others. That he shouldn't throw away whatever precious time he had left; he shouldn't drink it away.

I had to run from one end of the airport to the other to catch my connecting flight. They were waiting for me at the gate. I slapped my ticket into the man's hand and ran down a couple flights of steps out onto the runway. I had to duck my head as I boarded the twelve passenger puddle jumper.

The flight from Tampa to Denver had been smooth and uneventful as far as the flight was concerned. However, that was not the case from Denver to Durango. As we climbed to get over the mountains the plane's engines groaned, getting louder as we climbed. Not unlike a woman at the beginning of birthing. Generally, planes do not make me nervous, but I felt somewhat uncomfortable. Maybe it was a left-over feeling from my fellow passenger on the Denver flight. It was after the first range of mountains that all hell broke loose.

Lightening danced along the plane's wings. I could hear it sizzle as it snaked its way around the propeller. The rain, beast-like, pounded the plane, demanding entry into the cabin. Seven of us were on board: the pilot, co-pilot, stewardess, and four passengers. Three of the passengers, two women, and a man, each had single seats and were quiet. Winds continued to buffet the small plan. First one side and then the other. Back and forth. We were in a tennis match and we were the ball. Suddenly the plane gave a long tremulous shudder. The labor was intense now. We had dropped five hundred feet, straight down.

The man two seats in front of me lost it. What a mess! One of the women, the older of the two, began to pray aloud. The stewardess couldn't help the poor guy. She was buckled in, facing him. That certainly could not have been pleasant. The smell of his vomit assaulted my nostrils. Suddenly I realized the motors had changed; they were steady in their groaning. We were climbing again. The lightening had abated somewhat but the rain beat us relentlessly. The cross winds were unyielding.

Finally, the plane's captain announced we were making a final descent and to please keep the seatbelts fastened. I don't think anyone had unfastened them since take off. It was one hell of a ride down. Bumpy would be too mild a word.

Durango's airport looked about the size of a postage stamp, a misty yellow blob in the midst of a night of blackness made even blacker by the storm.

Our plane landed with a thud, and with a short taxi came to a stop. When we deplaned we had to slosh our way through gallons of water and pouring rain. The warmth of the small terminal was a welcome relief. I needed a drink, but first I checked on my transportation. A little man with an even smaller sign was pacing up and down in the small lobby. Once he stood still, I could see that his sign had my name on it, and it was written in small letters. Small is small I guess.

"I'm Adam," I said, walking over to the man.

"Your Cherokee is parked outside, gassed, and ready to go. Just sign here, please."

"Did you get the other stuff I requested?"

"Yes, sir. Everything for five days on the mesa. Here's the itemized list and the bill for that. Now if you'll just sign these."

"Not until I've checked the vehicle and made an inventory of the items I ordered."

I went out into the pouring rain, checked the jeep, started it up, and noted the gas gage read full. Next, I went through the boxes of items I had requested. It was as it should be. Satisfied, I signed the credit card slips, returning them to the little man, who patiently waited for me in the rain.

"You're sopping wet. Come on, I'll buy you a drink."

Back inside, I noticed the younger woman was also in the small bar. She was lip-locked with an older, gray-haired man. I ordered a brandy and the rental agency man ordered a shot of bourbon. There wasn't any talk. He downed his drink and got up to leave.

"Thanks for the drink."

"You're welcome. Sorry about the weather," I said, handing him a fifty. "For your time."

I sipped my brandy as I studied the map I had requested. The necking couple left, but not before kissing again at the exit. The old man's hands had free range over her not so subtle breasts. The man who had lost it on the plane emerged from the men's room. He was tall, handsome with long blue-black hair, a college kid. He had changed clothes. He had a certain swagger about him. Turning up the collar of his coat, he exited. I noticed he drove off in a car that had been parked next to my jeep.

Once I had finished my drink I hit the head and then got into the Cherokee turned the ignition. The engine fired and I headed toward the mesa and hopefully to Esaugetuh.

Carl Jung once wrote that modern man would never find peace unless he came to harmony with the place in which he lived. According to the literature I had gotten this meeting at Mesa Verde National Park was all about finding harmony. The line on its promo read, "The purpose of this spirit of place symposium is to better understand place consciousness and its role in helping modern science, design, architecture, and art recover their roots in nature and guide us to develop a sustainable society."

Roots? Place consciousness? Sustainable society? Whose? Where? Why? Man, that's what I call ambition! I thought as I sped along. I wonder what Esaugetuh is doing there? Maybe he's doing his shaman thing, whatever that is. Damn these one sided head conferences. They're always so dead end.

The road wound its way upward in a continual climb. Even though the rain had finally stopped the glare on the wet tarmac made it difficult to see. I slowed down. It was late when I arrived at the campground; just one person manned the registration station. I filled out the registration card, found my assigned slot, and backed the Cherokee in. I lowered the seat, pulled out my sleeping bag, crawled in and promptly went to sleep.

Soft spoken voices, coughing, and the smell of food woke me. It was still dark. I eased out of my sleeping bag, rolled it back up, opened the jeep's door, and caught the glimpse of what would be a spectacular sunrise. I hadn't slept long, but I still felt refreshed. More than I had in quite a while. I fished out a two-burner, pumped up the propane, and lit the hissing sound. Coffee would taste good, especially out here. Something about drinking coffee in the open air. I ate a couple of biscuits and downed two cups of coffee. By that time the sun had won its battle and lit up the bluing sky.

I went to the registration desk to ask about Esaugetuh. A different person was on the desk. Actually, it wasn't a desk, just a couple of stacked boxes under a large umbrella. The attendant wouldn't answer any of my questions until I showed my registration card. After that, I was given a polite 'no' to my inquiry. So he wasn't registered here. I drove up to the main lodge at the Park to check there. No luck. The clerk, however, suggested I check the motels in Durango and in nearby Cortez.

She was kind enough to give me the numbers of a couple of them. I had no better luck in that area either. Maybe my hunch was wrong, but I still felt it was correct. I just sensed that he had to be here.

Using the tourist-guide map of the Mesa Verde National Park, I decided to walk around. I drove up to the Park's entrance, left the jeep, and walked along the marked path to Spruce Tree-House, one of the many dwellings of the Ancient Ones. It felt good to be out. Gave me time to think. The quiet, broken by an occasional birdcall, seemed to refresh my soul. Maybe that what the Mesa does to you, like Colorado itself? The trees were different here and then there were the yucca plants. They were everywhere. One of the brochures remarked it was a staple among the early people.

What history is here? Hundreds of years before the white man. Hundreds? Hell, thousands of years. If these ruins, these rocks could only talk, I thought as I ambled along.

"But they do talk. The earth itself speaks. All you have to do is listen. Invite them and they will come."

It was Esaugetuh. I'd sure like to know how he gets into my head like that and answers my questions before I even verbalize them. However it is, I welcomed him warmly as I extended my hand even though I had a serious bone to pick with him.

CHAPTER ELEVEN
STILL AT THE MESA

Many things which cannot be overcome when they are together yield themselves when taken little by little.
Plutarch

"Why didn't you admit you were the one I was looking for? Why the god damned subterfuge? You know I've looked for you since I was a little boy? Why didn't you tell me you were leaving?" I yelled at him.

"Pissed are you?" Esaugetuh asked.

"Yes, I am. Damn pissed. I've spent months looking for you, nearly killing myself in the Canadian bush, driving hours on end, staying in a fee-bag of a motel, nearly bitten by a rattler, having the house around me shattered by some freakish storm, and then three thugs trying to wipe me out. Talk about being pissed. Oh, I'm pissed all right," I bellowed at him like some calf bawling for its mother.

"Three thugs, you say? When did that happen?" Esaugetuh said.

"Just as I was leaving the motel, right after I discovered you had split. Why?"

"Anything else strange happen on your trip here?" Esaugetuh asked.

"Other than one hell of a storm out of Denver nothing. Well, no, that's not true. I met this guy who said he was on his way to a funeral, his own. Gave me the creeps at first. Why?" I said, still very belligerent.

"Time will tell. But have you ever heard of patience, young fella? Youth! Always in a rush. And when it's gone they wonder where it went. Come walk me back to your vehicle." Esaugetuh said.

It was then that I realized that he was very old. Older than I had imagined him at the motel. I wondered how I could not have noticed. I felt really shitty about yelling at him. I felt guilty about keeping him up all hours of the night, totally disregarding his being. Showing a lack of respect at times. I sure wasn't aware. A real piece of work, that's what I am.

"I'm—,"

"No need to apologize," Esaugetuh said, cutting me off. "It's the nature of youth to be impatient with the old, and I have to admit, for the old to envy the young."

I drove him back to the campgrounds

"I've got things to do. I'll see you tonight after the ceremony, Esaugetuh said, getting out of the jeep.

With that, he disappeared into the crowd. I noticed that people stepped aside to make room for him as he walked. Even little children stopped their chatter and drew back, some clinging to their mother's legs while others stood with gapping mouths. Amazing! Absolutely amazing. He's so dignified, yet so humble. So damn real! Even the non-Indians hushed their voices. All I could do was watch and shake my head.

I spent much of the day roaming around the massive campsite. There were people there from most of the fifty states as well as several foreign countries. I guess they came to see the show, the creation of the great Medicine Wheel. I had never realized so many people were into this harmony thing. Oh, I remember reading about the 'convergence thing' from the days of the MacLaine movie [11] and the big deal that was supposed to happen in the Mayan jungles of Mexico. I was in Mexico at that time, but this—this has a different feeling about it. There really was a sense of spirit that required no special effects photography or background music to create a mood. It was the place itself and the people. They had a vitality reserved for those who relished life moment by moment. Those who were old had a certain air of renewal about them. And I envied all of them.

"Sir! Excuse me."

I turned to see who was speaking. It was the young man from the plane. He was as tall as I was, his long blue-black hair shone in the sunlight. I wasn't sure if he was a Native or a wannabe because he didn't have the identifying nose. The high cheek bones were present and seemed to accent dark brown eyes. A radiant smile crossed his open mouth.

"Sir weren't you just talking with the Old One?" he continued.

"Yes, do you know him?" I replied.

"Only by reputation. He speaks to very few people; even the chiefs back off in his presence. It seems strange to me that he should be speaking and riding with you since you are obviously not a Native American," he said with a slight edge to his voice.

Before I could reply another man ran up to him, whispered something and then both took off leaving me standing there. Not even an 'excuse me' from either of them. My instincts told me something was on the burner so I decided to follow them. After a meandering walk through pup tents, sleeping bags, conversion vans, pick-up trucks, and a wide variety of RV's, I came into a large clearing.

Several men sat cross-legged in a semi-circle facing a large group of seated people. At the center of these men sat Esaugetuh. He was regal, dressed in traditional regalia. Smoke curled up from his pipe as he slowly drew on it. His eyes were closed. Another elder was speaking. Suddenly Esaugetuh opened his eyes, looked directly at me, nodded, and then patted the ground beside him. I understood.

I made my way through the crowd, making sure I didn't step on anyone. A couple of times I got cussed because I brushed against them. When I got to the area where the elders were seated, Esaugetuh again patted the ground beside him. I sat down and as I did the man who was speaking stopped and looked down at me. A whisper rushed through the crowd, like a wave crashing upon a beach. Esaugetuh nodded to the speaker who then continued his story. As I listened to his native language I realized a literature was being spoken and eloquently at that.

I couldn't understand the language, but I knew, sensed, that something important was being said. The rhythmic patterns of his language, Navajo or Sioux perhaps, were truly beautiful, a song spoken. While he was speaking, I noticed another, younger man, standing. He was signing so those who could not hear could still read the words. I had taken a class in signing at the University but it was American Sign Language. Later I found out that he was telling the story of the Anasazi, the vanished people of a long ago civilization. As people left the circle I felt their hostility toward me. Esaugetuh had indicated I should stay seated. After an eternity of silence, he spoke.

"They do not hate you. They are afraid of you. They do not understand and what is not understood is often the source of fear. Do not concern yourself. Like time, it too will pass."

We got up. My legs were numb from sitting cross-legged for so long. Feeling gradually came back and we moved out of the clearing. Again, people stepped aside for Esaugetuh. As for me, I felt uncomfortable. Maybe it was real; maybe it was imagined. Whatever it was, it bordered the feeling you get when you're being watched.

"I'll see you tonight," Esaugetuh said, disappearing into the crowd.

"Damn!" I thought, "Why does he do that? Always when I'm about to ask a question. Wonder if he knew I wanted to go back to an earlier conversation. One thing is true; he holds power here."

Questions about his identity plagued me. As I arrived at my assigned campsite, I decided to drive up to the Lodge. It was a complex of several small cabins, a hotel, and a separate large restaurant. I parked the Cherokee and began to hike along the ridge to look for the famous Ship Rock. It took me awhile to focus, but there it was. A huge rock formation miles and miles away and the longer you looked at it the more it became an old sailing ship.

I sat down on the stone wall that ran along the path from the hotel and gave into the beauty that stretched out before me. The play of light on the rocks was hauntingly real. What tales they could tell! Stories of the people who had tread over them, migrating, ever moving onward. Onward? To where? What were their motivations? What were they seeking? What was their quest? Were they like me, always seeking? Wonder if they ever found answers.

The questions, always the questions. Will they never cease? I thought as I swung around to get down from the stone wall.

Standing there and watching me was the young man from the plane, the one and the same who had rudely walked off.

"Hope you don't mind if I followed you. I'm a reporter doing a story on the conference. I'd like to ask you a few questions if you have the time?" he said.

"I'm not sure why you'd want to interview me. There's certainly any number of well-known persons attending the conference. Wouldn't it be better to interview them?" I said.

"No, you're the one I want. You're the only Non-Indian who was asked to sit in the circle of teachers. That in itself is newsworthy, but who you are and how you know the Old One is of greater interest."

"Do you have a name?" I asked.

"I'm called Running-water. Sorry, I didn't introduce myself. And about leaving you back there, I'm sorry, but the story time was about to begin and I had been lead to believe the Old One would speak. I'd have hated myself if I had missed that. I work for a Rez rag and report on Native American activities."

"A Rez Rag?" I asked.

"Yeah. You know, an Indian Reservation newspaper. We call the Reservation, Rez," Running-water said.

I didn't realize that a newspaper was still referred to as 'rag' and its use threw me.

"Okay. I'm Adam."

"I know who you are, but not what you are," Running-water said flashing a picture-perfect smile.

"What do you mean by that?" I asked.

"Well, it's obvious you must be somebody pretty damn important to be seated at the Circle of Teachers but you must be somebody really important to be seated next to him, especially on his right side. Man, didn't you notice the stir you caused when you sat down next to the Old One?" Running-water asked.

"Of course I did. I assumed it was because I was interrupting the storyteller. Now there's someone you should be interviewing."

"I've already done that. So what's your connection to *him*?"

"I can't tell you anything about the old man, the Old One as you call him. All I know is that he calls himself Esaugetuh. Now if you'll excuse me, I have to meet a friend up at the Lodge."

"But—,"

I left him standing there and headed into the Lodge. I didn't want to talk about Esaugetuh. I had too many questions of my own that were begging for answers. Besides, whatever story there was, it was mine. I've been looking for him for years and I was not about to share his story with anyone. I went into the Lodge, looked around, found a side door, and slipped out. My drive back to the campsite was filled with more questions. As I backed into my assigned slot, Esaugetuh was waiting for me. He had something cooking in a black pot hung over an open fire.

As usual, I was hungry and ready to eat as he dished up a plate of stew. I told him about the reporter and as I explained my encounters with him, I noticed an unusual number of people slowing down as they walked by. Some stopped and stared. Esaugetuh interrupted my sense of discomfort.

"And what did you tell him?"

"What could I tell him? I know nothing about you. Where you come from? How old you are? Who your people are, or even what your name really is."

"You do not speak the truth," Esaugetuh said.

"Excuse me!" I said indignantly at his accusation.

"You know much about me. Have you not been researching this *me*? Have you not traveled into the Canadian bush, south to Florida, and now here to the Mesa just to be with me? Certainly one does not do all of this if nothing is known. Have you not learned anything about me from our conversations? The young Indian reporter knows all of this, also. He's been doing his homework. You are still too much with the material aspect of your personal quest. You are too interested in the phenomenon." Esaugetuh said.

"That's one of the many things I want to talk about, this thing you had called the noumenon."

"Not now. Eat. There'll be time for much talk after the Medicine Wheel."

Once I had finished my second plate, Esaugetuh gave me a Native homemade brew. It was sweet. Esaugetuh said it was made of corn mash and wild honey and a few other things he had thrown in. Biblically, I guess it would be pretty close to mead. Whatever the other ingredients were, I hadn't a clue.

"I've some things to do elsewhere. See to it that you get to the Ceremony and get there before it begins," Esaugetuh said as he left.

With nothing in particular to do, I decided to sack out for a while. When I woke up the sun had already set and darkness had begun to close in on the Mesa. A sprinkling of night-jewels, little diamonds, began popping into the clear Colorado sky. Sweetness filled the air, a delightful mixture of scrub pine, flowering sage bush, and various tobaccos of the pipe smokers. Because I thought the ceremony would be held at the same place where the story tellers had been, I went there. No one was there. A voice out of the darkness gave me direction. I followed and I soon came upon a large, round mud-brick structure. The moon was up and had given me a perfect outline. As I studied the image I noticed other shapes along the upper lip. A quick estimate would place the number at about two hundred. As I got closer to the kiva there was no question in my mind about the number of people there. Then it struck me that they were all men.

The reporter greeted me. Together we climbed up a makeshift ladder and eased our way around to the north center of the kiva's outer ring. I looked down into the massive hole. A small fire was burning just off center and along the outer circle, halfway round the wall, torches lighted the undefined face of an Indian man squatted beneath each torch. A yellow glow emanated from the kiva. From the air one would have the impression of a giant, glowing round saucer.

Several men in fancy Indian regalia sat in a semicircle just as they at the story time. In their center and at the exact center of the kiva was a sipapu, a shallow hole. It was my understanding that according to ancient tradition, it symbolized the site of the People's emergence. Out of a darkened part of the kiva and floating upward was a haunting, lilting melody of such beauty that tears came to my eyes. And I felt no shame in such emotion. Then all went quiet.

From the sipapu unfurled a lone figure, graceful and rhythmic in movement. The music once more filled the night air as the figure, fluid-like moved around the circle of light. It reminded me of Susan Seddon Boulet's painting, *Shaman,* a copy which still hangs in my office in New York. The dancing figure, cougar-like, stalked the center. Yet, eagle-eyed and all knowing the figure seemed to float back to the center from where it had first emerged. What a sight! The firelight showed white hair and just for an instant the azure blue eyes blazed and I knew it was Esaugetuh.

"What's the Medicine Wheel?" I whispered to Running-water, fearful of breaking the spell of the moment.

"It's called Circle of the Universe by some of the People. But whatever name it is called, it is a very special ceremony of harmony, of unification. My people believe that all living and non-living things are represented in that circle. Each man brings his totem, his symbol to the center. Each reflects the universe and the universe, in turn, reflects each thing like a mirror. Psychologists love to call them archetypes. Both ideas and beliefs are represented. Each seated man, in turn, will toss his symbol into the center fire, each becoming smoke, transcending to another, and going out into the universe itself, becoming one with that universe. A mirror of itself reflected upon itself. All being."

I was about to ask Running-water another question when he signaled for me to be quiet, to watch below.

"Something else is about to happen," Running-water whispered.

One of those who was squatted beneath the still burning torches stood up. He had a bow and a single arrow. He was naked except for a loin cloth; his skin shone in the flickering firelight. He tipped the arrow into the flame of the torch. It caught immediately. Masterfully he placed the arrow and pulled back. The bow arched and then he released it.

I nearly fell over the edge of the kiva and would have if Running-water hadn't grabbed me. The burning arrow landed right between my legs, too damn close for comfort. A rhythmical beat of hoop drums joined the singing flute. Suddenly all was silent. An owl hooted. The torches were extinguished and only the glowing embers in the center of the kiva remained visible. I sensed movement and then felt a tug on my arm.

"Come. It's over," Running-water said. "You have been much honored just the same."

"I don't understand," I said as we climbed down the old ladder. "What the hell's going on? What do you mean just the same?"

"Normally the man sought by the burning arrow would have been led down into the kiva, taken to its center, stripped naked to stand before the Nightwatchers and then receive the *ab*." [12]

"So what happened? Why wasn't I taken to the center to receive this 'ab' or whatever it is? My god, did you say naked?"

"A woman was discovered in the crowd and the sacredness of place had been violated. Women are not allowed at this kind of ceremony. Men have not known their women for several days before this ceremony. They have purified themselves through prayer, abstinence, and fasting. Women's time come later," Running-water said and then became silent.

"Look," I said, "Why me? I'm not a Native American."

"The Old One willed it. He directed the arrow," Running-water said.

"But why me?" I persisted.

"Ask him. When you find out let me know, okay? I'm out of here."

"Hey, where you going?" I asked.

"Got a date. See you."

I returned to the Cherokee, bedded down, and tried to go to sleep. A worthless effort.

CHAPTER TWELVE
THE PRECIPICE

Remain sitting at your table and listen ... simply wait, be quiet, still, and solitary. The world will freely offer itself to you to be unmasked, it has no choice, it will roll in at your feet.
Franz Kafka

Esaugetuh knocked on my jeep's side window. Night had not yet begun to give way to the advance of Helios. He wanted me to drive into the park. He assured me there would be no issue with the Park rangers. We arrived at a gate marked with a no entrance sign. Esaugetuh got out of the jeep, lifted the gate, and let it swing back wide. Then he motioned for me to drive through. He closed the gate and got back into the jeep. During our drive over a very narrow meandering road, he remained silent except for an occasional 'turn here.'

The early morning air was actually quite cold and for once I was glad I listened to my own advice and wore a heavier sweater. Colorado mountain air gets chilly at night and stays that way during the early morning hours. Jesus, it was only four-thirty. As we rounded a sharp curve we came upon a man standing along the road, oblivious to our presence. He was dressed in tattered jeans, flannel shirt, and a sleeveless vest. He had long straggly hair. Probably brown. Couldn't be sure. As I rolled down the window to speak to him I wondered what he was doing in a restricted area. He was sobbing, and he kept rubbing his eyes.

"Poor Yucca. Poor, poor Yucca. No one appreciates you anymore. It saddens me to see you neglected this way so I've come to be your friend. Don't you worry, little plant, I'll be your friend."

"There's a fool," Esaugetuh said.

That was the first full sentence he had spoken since we had left the conference camp grounds.

"He's a white man trying to be a Native. That's not the way you commune with the natural world. He's an insult to all of my aboriginal people," Esaugetuh said.

"I'm white and I'm just as aboriginal as anyone else is. Maybe not here but somewhere in this god damned world," I said, taking offense at his prejudicial comment.

It was all the more offensive because that was so out of character for Esaugetuh to speak that way. Oh, sure, he did not hold in terribly high regard those who were what he called the 'pretenders' or fakirs but making a racial comment was unusual.

"So you are! Turn right. Watch it. Stop!"

He had me pull the Cherokee into a narrow slit off the dirt road we were on. There was barely enough room to open the doors wide enough for us to get out.

"We walk from here," Esaugetuh said.

An hour later we were still climbing. I felt the altitude begin to take its toll. My breathing labored. Once I thought I heard a low growl but decided to keep it to myself. I did give my gun a pat, just for reassurance. Finally, we stopped. We were on a precipice. The view was spectacular, like those wide sweeping shots in the old western movies that had been filmed in Vistavision. A line from *America the Beautiful* popped into my head: 'O' beautiful for spacious skies . . . for purple mountain majesties above the fruited plain!'

Yes, purple mountain majesties but so much more. As I turned, the view on the opposite side was a giant paint box filled with coppers, some nearly golden while others were lavish oranges separated by dark purple shadows. No movie ever captured such splendor. Awesome seemed such an inadequate word to describe the panorama before me.

The climb had warmed me and I had to remove the heavy sweater I had on. I folded it and used it as a cushion. Esaugetuh remained standing, motionless, staring down into the deep canyon below. He straightened himself as he turned to face me. What a picture! Too bad I didn't have my camera with me. The morning sun shining through his white hair caught by a gentle breeze made the kind of picture advertisers try to create when making an anti-pollution pitch. You know the kind with a Native American standing or on horseback, a tear on his cheek. The difference, of course, was that Esaugetuh wasn't posing. He was totally natural, so completely a part of the world surrounding us. For a moment I felt he had always been there, transfixed throughout space and time—a reminder of that which had been.

"The world in which you and I are now in is not the only world. This planet we are on is like a large stage. Shakespeare was right when he said, 'All the world is a stage." A stage for Nature. Take, for example, the view that is in front of you. Look at it, smell it. That's sense experience. You see the magnificent colors and enjoy the multiplicity of their hues. You enjoy the nose tingling smells. But all of that is not enough," Esaugetuh said.

"What do you mean?"

"You—, and I mean you personally, want to know the meaning behind the experience; you want to know the thing within itself."

"The noumenon," I said.

"All physical events are spacio-temporal, that is, space, and time based. Everything in the material world happens within space and within a time sequence. You, however, want to experience that which can only be intuited. At least for now. You're right, of course, in sensing that there are some things you cannot experience with just your basic senses. The world you are so eager to know is indeed very much like Shakespeare's stage. Two realms intersect the one that is created, the one that is played out on the stage, and the one that is implied by that action on the stage. These 'strut their hour upon the stage . . ." And that's where he lost it. They don't 'strut their hour and heard no more.' They live forever in different realms," Esaugetuh said.

"Two realms? Explain," I said, leaning back on a rock to take better advantage of the rising sun.

"Yes. The spirit world and the human world, the material and non-material worlds, the sensed and the intuited worlds. The material world, the world of now, is all objects and they exist within space-time. But when you ask for meaning, answers cannot be given from the world of objects."

"Why not? We live in a world of objects," I said.

"Your material body, my material body, and all other material bodies in this world, including the universe itself, are intrinsically related and caught up in one single energetic event—creation—some call it the cosmological constant, an unknown form of energy. It's Taoism's 'Cradle of Immanence,' it's Christianity's 'Jesus Love,' the Kabbalah's 'Tree of Live,' it's Islam's 'Pure Allah,' it's Hinduism's 'Ineffable Brahman,' and in Buddhism it's 'The Noble Path.' I call it *fecundity*! The mind itself creates. All is creation! Look at the marvel before you. There she is, mother Earth, in all her magnificent splendor. It took millions of years to create this. Do you think She went to all of this work for all of those millions of years just to create you if there wasn't something She wanted you to do, some task, some purpose?"

"Your laying it on a bit heavy, don't you think?" I said.

"No. Rumi [13] put it this way, 'You have come into the world for a particular task, and that is your purpose.'

He sat down next to me, pulled out his clay pipe, filled it, and lit it. Then he offered it to me, saying, "When a pipe is offered, take it, smoke it, and return it to the giver."

After a bit, having seemed to have gathered his thoughts Esaugetuh continued, "Think about your evolution, of humankind's evolution. Why are you here? Just to breed? To pollute? To wage war? I think not. I certainly hope not! Another ancient people, those whom you call Sumerians, viewed themselves as caretakers of the earth, not as its owners. Ownership probably came about with the absurd notion of 'the divine right of kings.' Our mother, the Earth, has blessed you with certain creative powers that will come forth and blossom when it's time for you to do her work. Just as this view unfolds before your eyes, there will be an unfolding of your creative powers. It is She who awakens this unfolding, a vision of you as energy—aware of itself as Self—creative, and full of power. Perhaps another analogy."

He bent over, picked a dandelion, held it up to me, and slowly turned it between his fingers.

"Take this dandelion. It's a common, ordinary wild flower that many view as a noxious weed, a nuisance. Yet, it opens, unfolds itself to all there is, accepting and giving, an intercourse with the universe. As its seeds and forms a perfect sphere does it not reflect the totality of that universe? That's its purpose. To accept, to give, to mirror and if you examine each of its seeds you will find replication, a mirrored image of its Self. Are you less a mirrored image of that same universe?"

"Okay, I'm supposed to have a purpose. How do I know what the hell that is? What my Self is for that matter? This mirroring you speak of is confusing," I said.

"Begin by observing the world around you. Open all of your senses to all that there is. Drink it in, sponge-like. Become sense-aware. Notice the great eagle soaring above? Even now he speaks to you, as did the snake to me. Listen."

"I heard its call. Nothing else," I said.

"Not just with your ears. Listen with your soul-self. Always the soul-self. It's the connection. Lean back on that rock, close your eyes, still yourself. Empty your mind of all thought."

I did as he directed. The longer I laid there the less I heard, ending up with hearing the thump-thump of my own heart. Nothing more. Suddenly I felt very foolish and my face flushed hot. Was I being had? Is this old man, himself a fakir?

Esaugetuh must have sensed my building doubts because he abruptly said it was time to leave. We did. The hike back to the jeep was a lot easier than the climb up. Nothing more was said. It was plain to see he was totally disgusted with me.

"Look," I said, "I can't hear what I don't and I can't see what I don't even though I wish, with all my heart, that I could."

As he got out of the jeep he said, "Focus your mind on one thing, and absorb its qualities, its attributes."

He was gone!

CHAPTER THIRTEEN
OUR MOTHER EARTH

A day like today I realize what I've told you a hundred different times—that there is nothing wrong with the world. What's wrong is our way of looking at it.
Henry Miller
(A Devil in Paradise)

You wonder sometimes, don't you? I mean about the number of terrible natural disasters that happen. Makes you stop and ask what this old world of ours is coming to. The horrendous tsunamis that struck Indonesia and India, the hurricanes that wiped out parts of Florida, Louisiana, and Mississippi, the tremendous forest fires in the midwest and western parts of the United States, tornadoes, flooding, blizzards, earthquake destruction in Haiti, and the eruption of volcanoes certainly cause you to wonder.

Why does a twister take one house and not another? Why is one life taken and not another? Thornton Wilder tried to answer that one. Remembering the destruction of my motel cabin in Florida caused me to shudder. No matter how hard I tried I couldn't shut down that damn conference going on in my head. It was just like a bowling alley. Every time a row of pins were set up, they were knocked down. Every time I thought I understood something I found I didn't. Restless probably should be my name. Just as I finally began to doze off I heard him.

"Our Mother Earth is awakening to her own power and future potentialities. She is awakening to an ever unfolding vision, a vision of a self-aware entity."

"Esaugetuh, where in hell are you? What's with this cloak and dagger stuff?" I said as I sat up in my sleeping bag. "Just a damn minute. I'll light the lantern."

"Don't bother with a lantern. Where I am is unimportant. What I have to say is. Other ears cannot hear my voice so don't worry about disturbing others."

"Okay, so what's so god damned important that you had to wake me up, especially when I had just gotten to sleep?"

"Stop complaining. First of all, I appreciate the fact that you didn't pretend to hear the Eagle speak to you. I would have known you were faking it. That speaks well for you."

"No problem," I whispered.

"Pay attention to what I am about to say!" Esaugetuh was adamant.

"Earth is cleansing her being of the ugliness that has come upon her. She is casting out the stuff that has harmed her, polluted her rivers and streams, and polluted her air and vegetation, and polluted her humans. Gaia will destroy all humankind before she allows the pollution to continue."

"I've read all of that somewhere before," I said disinterestedly.

"I don't mean to infer that we will experience Armageddon or that everything will be vaporized. The lowly cockroach serves as an example of survival. And I'm not suggesting an apocalypse in the current usage of that word. At this very moment, humanity is racing into a new realm, a new era. Some have called it Millennium, some the Age of Gaia, while others have called it Noosphere. Whatever name is used, each entity will be understood as part of a total community, a fabulously pregnant womb of the creative life—fecundity at its best."

"You woke me just to tell me that we are going to survive like the cockroach? Oh! Great! Just great! What the hell has that got to do with me?"

"Simply this. Earth Mother awakens to the human mind. Humanity is the consciousness of the earth and whether or not you believe it, you personally are a part of that transforming consciousness. Further, your human heart is capable of loving all things without strain, capable of housing great empathy, of sharing that sense of life itself. It's within this framework that you will continue your very personal quest. At this moment, Adam, you are more emptiness than self-aware of Self. It is the soul-self that you must change. A self-aware of Self is a necessary condition for love, a necessary condition for survival. Love is one of the essential attributes of Selfhood.

I'm talking about much more than sensual pleasures, and they do have their place and value, don't misunderstand. I'm talking about a love that means giving value to all that exists, beginning with the self, and extending that worth to all things big and small, living and non-living. The potential for you to love all existence is limited only by your refusal to achieve all the attributes of Selfhood. I say refusal because that also means a rejection of the value of Self and that condemns you to a depraved agony and a mode of self-destruction, which produces nothing more than an automaton. As you achieve these attributes one by one you will realize the last is the least difficult to achieve and it will arrive more silent than sea fog rolling in across the land. And like that fog, it will engulf you, totally and completely, bathing you in a newfound realization that only a genuine sense of Self can provide," Esaugetuh said.

"What kind of shit are you feeding me now?"

Ignoring my sarcasm, Esaugetuh continued, "When you realize and understand that there are patterns in your life, everyone's life, for that matter, and Joseph Campbell wasn't wrong here, then you will fully understand that you are engaged in a global, no, a universal unfolding drama, cosmic in its very nature. An exquisite drama of the soul, the self-same soul that you have always been taught was reserved only for the saints or for the gods, and on very rare occasions, for the heroic martyr."

I yawned. I didn't mean to, but I did. And I was sure I had been heard and that I probably have added insult to injury. The air here is different than Florida and I've not acclimated yet. I didn't hear anything, and thinking that he had left in a pout I said, "You still there? Say something."

"Yes, I'm still here. What has been so clearly left out is that you and all the others in this world are deity in posse. You are eternal and universal, parallel, implicate, and explicate, dynamic and simultaneous. Unfortunately, you are bifurcated. No matter the metaphor, there is the sameness everywhere, from the Age of the Golden Ones to the Prometheans, to the first man, and now in this time, the Coming of New Adam," Esaugetuh said.

"Why do you say unfortunately bifurcated? Don't we live in a world of duality? Man and woman, sweet and sour, high and low, hot and cold, good and evil. Even Biblically we are told Noah brought two's on board his Arc."

"You've missed the point. Take good and evil, which you mentioned. Actually, they are of the same stock—forked, thus appearing to be two different entities, but they are still the same just as you and I are of the same root. Think of it this way. A river and all of its tributaries or branches contain the same water flowing through them yet we have given each a separate name. Naming doesn't make them different. Modern man has attempted to change all of this with his millions and millions of laws. Even his religions with all of their do's and don'ts, shall and shall-nots have attempted to identify two different aspects of the one. That's why they are failures! In creating this unnatural duality they have made demands clothed as grand promises and always wanting something in return as payment."

"A payment," I quizzed.

"Well, yes. Where's there's a promise made it is done so only when something is to be given in return. I'm sure you remember times when one or both of your parents promised to do something if you did something first. Oh, if you got good grades they promised you a new bike."

"Sure, but what kid hasn't had that experience? I guess I still don't get it."

"Those who make promise-demands do so in order to maintain control. To hold power and to stay in power they must keep others in ignorance, that is, will they or won't they withdraw their promise. The ignorant are always afraid that they individually will be sacrificed, and because they don't know, they will be obedient. That is, they surrender their individuation, that Self-same Self I've been talking about. Keeping the sacrificial lamb in ignorance is essential to those who claim power. Didn't the great Greek warrior-hero, Agamemnon, keep his own daughter in the dark as he prepared to sacrifice her? In the Christian world, didn't their God keep Abraham ignorant of the lamb that he was to sacrifice in place of his son, Isaac?

"So now what?" I said.

"Sylvanus said it best, 'Open the door for yourself that you may know what it is.'"

"Are you inside or outside of the jeep?" I asked.

"I am."

I thought I heard a slight rustle and felt a cool breeze fill the jeep. Yet I didn't hear the door open or close. I withdrew deeper into the womb of my sleeping bag, unable to go back to sleep, I waited for the morning.

CHAPTER FOURTEEN
MORNING

Every morning is a new arrival. Be grateful for whoever comes, because each has been sent as a guide from beyond.
Rumi

I woke up thinking that the earth is definitely being transformed and it's being transformed because it's alive, alive because it has a soul. I guess what Esaugetuh was trying to get me to understand was that if I could grasp the soulness of the world I'd understand the language of things. I rolled out of the sleeping bag and out of the jeep expecting to find Esaugetuh. He was gone! I walked along the rows of campers. No one seemed to know anything about him or who it was I was looking for. No one by the name of Esaugetuh existed. I was given the same type of shut-out I got in Canada.

"Damn!" I was hot.

Then why should anyone tell me anything? Am I not the interloper? Now what? I spent the remainder of the day looking for him. As nightfall approached I decided to pack it in and head back to Durango. I called and booked a flight back to Denver and then out the next day to New York.

I headed southeast toward Durango and as I was winding my way down the mountain I spotted a car off the road in a ditch. Recognizing Running-water I pulled over and stopped.

"A blow-out. It was either the ditch or the cliff. Can you give me a lift? There isn't a jack or spare in the trunk. Hell of a note, don't you think. You rent a car you'd think it'd have the necessary equipment in it."

"I got a jack, but since you don't have a spare tire it won't do you any good. I'm headed into Durango. Hop in. You can have the car picked up and get a different one. This time, check to make sure it has a spare tire and a jack. And by the way, make sure the spare has air in it," I said, as I eased the Cherokee back onto the road.

"Thanks. You always such a mother hen?" Running-water said, grinning from ear to ear.

"Esaugetuh has disappeared on me again. And no one, not one god damned person would say anything about him. They even pretended they didn't know who I was talking about. Really pisses me off. Say, you don't happen to know where he's headed to you?"

"I'm not sure where's he gone. Since you've picked me up, I'll tell you what I know as payment for the ride," Running-water said.

Something that Esaugetuh had said about promises and payments popped back into my head. In fact, it slapped me in the face.

Continuing, Running-water said, "I'd sure like to know your connection to him. What is he to you? Is he a relative?"

"I'm not a relative. I believe he's a very powerful shaman, a man of great mystery. I believe he's from Canada. I'm a freelance writer and I've been working on a piece about shamanism among

Native Americans and First People of Canada. It was my understanding that Esaugetuh if that's really his name, would be a good study."

"And that's all?"

"I suppose there's more. Always is, isn't there? Since meeting him he has become my mentor. Right now, however, I'm not sure what the hell he is."

Leaning back in his seat, Running-water said, "It's pretty obvious that you're very special, especially to him."

"What's that supposed to mean?"

"Well, a man of his stature, a person of his renown, and power just don't go around holding special ceremonies for just anyone let alone a white man."

"I'll be damned. A special ceremony. What kind of ceremony was that last one we were at?" I asked.

"It was a ceremony of succession," Running-water replied, pleased with himself.

"Successor? What kind of successor?" I asked.

"The Old One has adopted you and has chosen you to carry on for him. And since he has adopted you, you are now recognized as his son."

"But didn't the ceremony end because of some violation? If that's true, then am I to assume this adoption thing didn't go through?"

"No. The arrow chose you. You just didn't get presented, officially."

"I'll be damned."

"You already said that."

"So I did."

I pulled into the car rental agency and left Running-water there to haggle over his leased car. I headed on into the airport terminal to cancel my flight to Denver and New York. I booked a flight to Seattle instead. Running-water said he had heard Esaugetuh talking to tribal members from Washington. I paid for my ticket and waited to board. I hoped the flight would be better than the one coming in. I would have a connecting flight out of Albuquerque to Seattle. A two hour lay-over would give me time to do some much needed reflection.

Socrates demonstrated that you know the answers if the right questions are asked. I guess I've not been asking the right questions. So, what are the right questions?

Okay, first question. Why me? My god, a shaman. No. No way!

CHAPTER FIFTEEN
SEATTLE

Away with the one who is always seeking, for he never finds anything; for he is seeking where nothing can be found. Away with the one who is always knocking, for he knocks where there is no one to open; away with the one who is always asking, for he asks of the one who does not hear.
Tertullian

Well, here I am just off another plane. I guess good old Tertullian was right. I am always seeking, but I never seem to find anything. Always asking, but never getting an answer. Maybe Esaugetuh or whatever his name is, isn't the one to ask. I've had that experience before. Maybe that's why he disappears. Maybe there are no answers!

As I sat there in the airport at Albuquerque just for a second I thought I saw Running-water hurrying by. He wasn't such a bad guy, just a bit brash. Not any more than I am. I spent my time watching people. Some were running to catch a flight, others were being greeted, and some were strolling along without an apparent care in the world. Others were talking non-stop on their cell phones. As I watched them it occurred to me that none of them realized the existence of anyone else. If they did, it was only because they got in their way. I paid particular attention to the women. Some were harried mothers with kids in tow, others were the macho-business women their aggressiveness all too obvious, and then there were a few who were overly made up, greeted by some older guy, or in some cases, by older women. It was easy to determine their line of work.

Whoa!" I thought, "We sure are being judgmental. Time to knock that crap off.

Then I remembered the man I met on the plane flying into Denver. I wondered if George Talbot was still alive. I pulled out my cell phone and called Denver Information. Once I had the number I punched it in. On the fifth ring I was about to hang up, but a woman's voice answered.

I asked to speak to George. I reminded him who I was and where we had met. Then I asked him how he was. His reply nearly knocked me out of my seat.

"I'm fine. Never felt better in my life. Had a physical yesterday, and absolutely no sign of the tumor. Funny you should remember. I sure remember you though. I remember what you had said to me," George said.

"You've got me there. But I am glad you're okay. That's great news!"

"You asked me how I was going to live the rest of my life. Well, I added, how was I going to live the rest of my life. And when I answered that I found life to be beautiful, rich, and rewarding. And it's all because of you. What is your name?"

"Adam. So what are you doing now?"

"I spend my days at the local hospitals with kids who have cancer. I teach them self-hypnosis to help them control their pain."

"Good for you. That's great. Look, my plane is boarding so I have to go. Good luck."

"Same to you."

The plane was nearly filled to capacity. This time, even though I had requested a window seat, I didn't get one. I dislike being in the middle. Maybe I'm claustrophobic. I remember a time on my way to Boston and I was seated between to very large men. We hit some rough weather and the stewardess took my drink away. I broke out in a cold sweat. I felt that if something happened I wouldn't be able to move out of my seat because the men were so large. After reaching our designated altitude the stewards began to come by with refreshments. I was going to order a double.

"Excuse me. Adam?"

"Yes. Is there a problem?" I asked.

"No, sir. The captain would like to know if you would care to move to first class. We have a vacancy there."

"Hey buddy, if you're not going to take it I will," said a man seated on the outside aisle.

"I'm sorry sir, the offer is extended only to Adam," the steward said.

"Thanks. And tell the Captain thank you. I just need to get my backpack," I said.

I wasn't sure why I was advanced to first class. It was nice. When I got to my new seat, I was handed a note in a sealed envelope. I opened it and was surprised. It was from George Talbot. It simply said, 'Thanks. You saved my life. Enjoy your trip.'

"I'll be damned," I said aloud.

"Good news, I hope."

The voice belonged to the woman seated across the aisle from me. She was probably in her late seventies, fashionably dressed, and sipping a glass of wine. The laugh-lines suggested she enjoyed herself, however, the dent in the middle of the forehead, just above her ever so slightly turned up nose suggested otherwise; that things are not as they appear to be.

"Yes. It is good news. My transfer to first class status was a surprise gift. Thank you for asking," I said.

"Do you mind if I join you? I so hate sitting by myself."

I indicated that would be fine. As she got up, the stewardess appeared and helped her change seats. I noticed she had a badly swollen left leg. It had a bluish pallor about it.

"Thank you. I'm Delilah Geoffrey. Hope my bum leg doesn't offend you. I'm on my way to a hospital in Seattle. Hopefully, they can do something about it. Ghastly thing that it is."

"The cause of the swelling hasn't been determined," I asked.

"No. I told them I thought I was bitten by an insect. But my doctors couldn't find any indications of a bite. I guess by that, they couldn't find a point of the bite or a point of festering. Would you mind holding my glass for me while I fish around in my handbag? I'm always afraid of spilling," Delilah said.

Once she had retrieved whatever it was she wanted, I handed back her glass of wine. I was sure she had the glass in her hand. Anyway, the wine went all over her leg. I'm not sure which one of us was more embarrassed. In trying to wipe up the spilled wine, I realized that her left leg was hot to the touch. She didn't seem to notice that I had touched her.

It was not a long flight into Seattle. As we approached, the Captain announced Mount Rainier was visible. I looked out my window. Rainier was definitely the mighty sentinel, glowing in the evening sunlight. It was Heliodoric. I had forgotten that Washington stays light longer into the evening than the rest of the forty-eight contiguous states during the summer months. The snow cap sparkled like a precious jewel in a showcase.

Once we had landed, the stewardess helped Delilah into a wheel chair.

"Thank you for putting up with this old lady," Delilah said, giving me a wave.

"What hospital are you going to?" I asked.

"University. Be there for a few days."

"Good luck. If the doctors can't do it, heal yourself," I said as she was wheeled away.

After deplaning and picking up my luggage I rented a vehicle and headed north toward the Canadian border. Washington is the home for a number of different Indian tribes, all of which have their own governance. Among those that would be northbound are the Swinomish, Snohomish, Lummi, Makah, and Tulalip. Just maybe that old fox was heading back into Canada and I wondered if he might be trying his luck at one of the casinos.

I whipped the rental off I-5 and pulled into a casino. It was not a new one. The building was nothing, in particular, to look at, no Indian sculptures, fountains, or gardens to give it appeal. I parked the car and headed toward the entrance. A large man greeted me at the door. I noticed several men of the same stature walking the grounds. A nice touch. To protect the winners or losers? Not sure which. Probably both. Inside, I took my time to look around the large open gaming room. Electronic slots whined as people punched the play buttons. Evidently, I was taking a little too much time.

"Excuse me. You need some help?"

The voice belonged to one of the men I saw patrolling the grounds. There was no smile with the greeting. Strictly business.

"As a matter of fact, yes you may. I'm looking for a friend. I was supposed to meet him. I don't see him. Perhaps you know him? He's a Native American like you."

"This friend got a name?"

"He is called Esaugetuh by some," I replied.

The room quieted so much it startled me. I looked at the man who had asked if I needed help. His face was that of stone, no expression. Players weren't pushing the buttons on the machines. They were too busy staring in my direction. I felt very uncomfortable. I fought an urge to turn and run; yet I stayed, frozen by the silence of the moment. Before I could turn I felt a hand on my shoulder.

"Come," Esaugetuh, said.

Obediently I followed. As at the Mesa, people stepped aside as he approached. What a sight he was: skin glowing bronze, white hair in double braids tumbling down over his broad shoulders and coming to rest on his expansive chest. A single eagle's feather, painted on the tip, toped his hoary crown. Of course, his azure blue eyes brought people to him. They couldn't look away. The white suit with its golden beads punctuated his whole golden being, showing off a lean muscularity. His shirt, open at the neck, revealed a small leather pouch hanging on a leather string. At that moment, I believe each person in the main room saw in Esaugetuh what they wanted to see—what they believed to be a divine reality. His being filled the whole casino. A movie director could not have staged a better scene.

We turned down a dimly lit corridor and came to stop in front of a door guarded by a young man with long black hair tied in a single braid. He nodded to Esaugetuh and opened the door, and then stood aside. Esaugetuh indicated that I was to follow. It was a room used by high rollers, tastefully decorated in dark mahogany table and bar. Chairs were done in Moroccan red leather. Hanging on one wall, in a glided gold frame, was a large picture of Chief Seattle. The room was windowless and appeared to have just the one door, the one through which we entered.

Esaugetuh walked over to a mahogany credenza, taped out his pipe in a glass ashtray, and picked up a very expensive looking crystal decanter. He seemed to ponder over the choice of glasses, finally selecting a pair of stemmed ponies. He poured a drink into each.

"Brandy. Good for you. You look terrible. You okay?"

"What's with this find me if you can game? What the hell was all that shit back at the Mesa? I want explanations and I want them now!"

"Well, don't you have an attitude? Okay, I'll begin with you. Why are *you* here? Why are *you* following me? What is it *you* want from me? You are stalking me?"

"You know damned well why I'm following you. And don't start that ten and twenty question routine with me either," I said, really pissed.

"Now who's playing games?" Esaugetuh said, sipping his brandy. "It's not me you are after. You know it and I know it. I'm merely a tool for your use. Something to be used to further your own ends. The real issue is whether or not you are willing to come to grips with the truth."

"The truth! What the hell do you think we've been talking about?" I was livid.

"Your truth. The truth of your Self, of your being, of your existence."

"That's not a revelation. You knew from the very beginning I had questions and I was trying to find their answers. What's wrong with my being on a quest?" I growled.

"The Ancient Ones would tell you that it is wrong if you cannot identify the nature of your quest. I tell you, you are wrong. You have not named your quest," Esaugetuh said.

"Okay, so I'm on a quest and I haven't given it a name. So what?"

"For starters, it is a big deal, a very big deal! Unless you identify the nature of your quest it will be a failure. I'm trying to prepare you for that possibility. In your soul, you know that and that is the real reason you continue to follow me and it's also the real reason why you are angry, angry because I know. And all of this is part of your quest. The arrow has spoken.

"The arrow you had shot at me nearly made me a eunuch. So, what was all that arrow business anyway? Running-water, the Indian reporter, told me it was a ceremony to choose your successor?"

He had me and he knew it. I looked directly at him, searching his face for a clue. I tossed down the brandy. It was smooth.

"I did not have the arrow shot at you. If you will recall, it was shot straight up into the air. The spirits willed its direction. Yes, it was a ceremony of selection. The spirits have willed it. I am to be your guide—but you still have not identified your quest—because you haven't, I can't reveal any more than I have. There is only so much I may say. You have to declare, to make it, and then you must reveal its nature. That is your obligation," Esaugetuh said.

"I can't. I don't know what the hell it is. I have this god-awful gnawing in my gut. It never goes away. I have questions and more questions. But no answers. Sometimes I think I'm insane, a lunatic who has escaped from some bizarre institution. Maybe Tertullian was right. Maybe I am the one who is always seeking and the one who never finds anything," I said.

"No, my young friend you are not crazy. Be patient. Strange and wondrous things have been happening. A white buffalo has been born; a pure white cow with curly hair has been birthed, a white robin has been spotted. Now I hear that a second white buffalo has been born. The new age has begun. And you—you are its precipitator. Tomorrow you will see another strange event."

"Another strange event?"

"Yes. Didn't you notice the huge ring around the sun today and that a second ring joined it? Very strange. Tomorrow."

With that, he left the room. The young man with the braid stepped into the room and indicated that I should leave. I did.

I drove to a motel, took a room for the night. Ordered a burger and fries to be sent to my room. Somehow I knew that Esaugetuh would be waiting for me in the morning. I'm not sure about being his successor. True, it's a cool idea, but I'm not sure what it involves. I had barely gotten out of the shower when my burger and fries arrived. I woofed them down with a pop. The bed felt good and I soon was asleep.

CHAPTER SIXTEEN
ON THE SKAGIT

Seek and inquire about the ways you should go, since there is nothing else as good as this.
The Gnostic Gospels

A phone message from Esaugetuh said he'd meet me after breakfast and that we'd head up the Skagit. The Skagit, as it turned out, was a 150 mile long river that wound its way from southwestern British Columbia into northwestern Washington; there dumping into Skagit Bay, an inlet of Puget Sound. Its valley blossoms with hundreds of acres of tulips in the spring, and gleams with snow-capped mountain views in winter and summer. It is the feeding ground for the great bald eagle and dozens of different migratory birds.

I scanned a local paper while waiting for Esaugetuh. One item caught my eye. A bald eagle had been killed—struck by lightning on some island off the coast of Washington. There was a picture of it in a death grip on a tree limb. I'd never heard of a bird being struck by lightning before. Strange! The paper said its remains would be shipped to Colorado to a national archive for eagles.

Bet that cost the taxpayers a pretty penny.

Only Native Americans, by Federal law, are allowed to possess eagle feathers. The reason behind this is that the feathers are used in many of the religious rituals carried on by the Indians. As I sat at my breakfast table mulling over this bit of information, Esaugetuh appeared and as usual, he appeared from out of nowhere. He was anxious to get started and directed me to a sporting goods store. There he selected a wide range of items, beginning with a small two-man skiff, a pop-up tent, a couple of cooking pans, and utensils, and blankets. Our next stop was at a food store. He had me get just a few basic staples: salt and pepper, cooking oil, and coffee.

When he got back into the rented jeep, a Cherokee, he told me to take a two-lane and head north. It meandered through great farm country, flat land with rich dark soil, the kind that's good for growing vegetables. Not many animals other than a few cows here and there. The earth, green-fresh with furrows of dark soil showing between the rows of new growth, made the snow-capped mountains even more majestic as they reached skyward, purveyors of all that exists. In the distance, I noticed a large field of pure white and it seemed to be moving.

"What the hell's that?" I asked.

"Trumpeter Swans."

"Must be thousands of them," I said, slowing the jeep so I could get a better view.

Anticipating my next question Esaugetuh said, "They came down from the far north for the winter. They'll head back soon, some to give birth, and others to die."

"Whew! That's a morbid thought," I said.

"It's time," Esaugetuh said.

"Time for what? Death?"

"Time that we stopped thinking of life as an abstraction with a footnote called death to which all things are eventually appended, a negative thing. Rumi, the Persian poet, put it this way when he wrote:

I died as a mineral and became a plant,
I died as a plant and rose to animal,
I died as an animal and I was Man.
Why should I fear? When was I less by dying? [14]

It's time that you begin to see the essence of things—their energy and to understand that energy—that it is everlasting, a totality of experience and since it is, then this thing we call life cannot be the whole story. Remember, in order to delight in your own Selfhood you must first delight in the existence of all other things—even the potentiality inherent in death as Rumi stated so very well, 'When was I less by dying?'"

"And just how am I supposed to see this essence of all things?"

"First, and this is very important, you must rid yourself of those pre-conditioned aspects of your perception. You must learn to look at things through new eyes. You must be mindful. Pull over and stop."

I pulled the jeep to the side of the road. Esaugetuh's use of mindful set off a bell. I remembered Delilah Geoffrey.

"Excuse me; I need to make a phone call. It'll just take a few minutes."

I whipped out the cell phone, brought up 'Information' and asked for the university medical center. Man, talk about going through your paces. I thought I'd never get anywhere. The privacy laws can be a royal pain in the ass. Finally, I had to pretend to be Delilah's attorney. They connected me. She was ecstatic.

"You know Adam, I believe it's all your doing," Delilah said.

"My doing?"

"Yes. You told me to heal myself. That's what I did. My leg is nearly normal. I'm going home tomorrow."

"I'm happy for you. Take care," I said.

"You got a woman you've not told me about?" Esaugetuh asked, nudging me with his elbow as I turned off the cell phone.

"No. She was someone I met on the plane on my way out here. Her left leg was badly swollen. She said doctors didn't know what was wrong with her. Now she tells me her leg is healed."

"Is that all she said?" Esaugetuh asked his curiosity showing.

"She said it was my all my doing."

"Your doing?" Esaugetuh asked.

"That her leg healed."

"Interesting. Maybe there's hope for you after all. Get out of the jeep."

We got out of the jeep. I walked around to the passenger side where Esaugetuh was standing and pointing up at the sky.

Esaugetuh said, "What do you see?"

"A bunch of birds flying around."

"That's your old pre-conditioned perception responding. Look again. What kind of birds? How are they flying? What colors do you see? Are some birds larger than others? Are they all the same kind?"

I looked again, straining to see details. There were about a dozen large birds, dark in color, white on their heads, and white tipped feathers. The tips of their wings curved slightly upward as they circled lower and lower. Then one made a dive toward the river. Swoosh! It had a fish.

"Bald eagles. Those with white heads are mature birds. Now look into the trees," Esaugetuh said.

I looked. First I saw nothing, and then as I focused I saw them. Large dark spots sitting on branches, high up. More eagles. What a sight! Before an hour was up I had counted a good two dozen eagles.

"Was a time you could see hundreds. But that's another story. Look along the river's far bank and tell me what you see," Esaugetuh said.

"Trees."

"Wrong answer. What kind of trees? What color, shapes, and sizes?"

"How am I supposed to know all that shit, for Christ's sake? A tree is a tree. I'm not a god damned botanist."

"Look again. Are they all the same?" Esaugetuh said ignoring my obvious frustration.

"No. Some are—,"

"And people? Are they all the same?"

"Of course not," I said, becoming more annoyed at playing school. Why can't he just get to the point? Cut to the chase.

"But to you, they are just birds, just trees, and just people. There is no delight in your recognition of their existence and because there is none, you cannot take delight in your own existence. When you wished the woman good luck there was no genuine interest in your voice. I actually wondered why you bothered to call her. Was she just 'people'? Maybe I've turned out to be 'just people'?"

"That's not fair,"

One more example and then we'll make use of that inflatable skiff you brought along. Look at the mountain on the other side of the river and tell me what you see."

"A mass of green."

"And what do you see when you see green?"

"Do you mean the color green?" I protested.

"What do you really see when you see green?" Esaugetuh repeated.

"Yellow and blue."

"Now you're beginning to catch on. Look beyond. See beyond. What effect does the yellow have on the blue? What effect did the woman with a leg problem have on you? What effect did the man who had cancer have on you? What effect does love have on a human being? All of this is the noumenon you were so interested in, that thing-in-itself, that which lies behind the experience. To achieve that understanding you must first change your way of looking and of seeing. We can make use of that skiff now," Esaugetuh said.

I hauled the skiff down to the water, stashed in our gear and with Esaugetuh set out for a small sandbar out in the middle of the river. It was more strenuous than I had imaged because the river was fast moving, no lazy river this one. I would have overshot the sand bar had Esaugetuh not finally picked up an oar and helped. He maneuvered the skiff with simple short strokes. We hit the sand bar with a thud. He was the first one out, secured the skiff and had me handing him the supplies. Pitching the tent was my assignment. I was glad it was one of those two-man pop ups. I made short work of staking it down.

Esaugetuh had made a small hole in the ground. He placed an unopened can of brown beans in its center. Then he punched two small holes in its top. Next, he built a small fire over the can of beans. While the beans were heating he made what he called flat bread out of corn meal and put that in a frying pan. As soon as the coals were really hot, he sat the pan of bread to cook. He handed me the coffee pot.

"Fill it with water from the river."

Once I had the water, he filled its basket with coffee. I noticed he had poured some of the water out. In answer to my quizzical look, he said, "Don't want to get the coffee wet before it perks. Makes bitter coffee."

The beans and cornbread disappeared within short order. I didn't realize I was hungry. I also noticed that he had used just one can of beans for the two of us. Small portions equal lean body.

As the sun set the temperature dropped. The small fire offered little in the way of real warmth. The coffee had perked. Esaugetuh poured us each a cup and laced each with a generous finger of brandy. It helped keep the chill away.

Night had finally pulled its shade. The swirling sound of the river rushing headlong to it destiny created a hypnotic rhythm. Its sound was broken by an occasional whirr of a bird's wings. As we sat there a flash of light slashing the night sky caught my attention. As I continued my upward gaze, the nothingness of the darkness turned into millions of gleaming little dots. Those became stars as I focused; millions of stars, no billions of winking eyes. What a view! The mountains, acting as a shielded telescope, emphasized the larger dots that seemed to swirl upward and outward at the same time. It was beautiful! As I squinted my eyes Van Gogh's painting, *Starry Night*, came to life.

His voice barely above a whisper Esaugetuh asked," What do you see up there?"

"Stars. Billions of stars," I said.

"What else? Remember, look beyond."

"I see a vastness, shades of black, constellation shapes," I said.

"And light?" Esaugetuh asked.

"Yes, from the stars."

"That light is very old; the stars that produced it have already burned out. You are looking at an ancient history, at what was and what is simultaneously. It's past-present. If past-present can exist, so too, can present-future. Always remember that, Adam. Each star is a cell in the cosmic brain just as we humans are, just as is every living thing. Pretty marvelous, don't you agree."

"Yeah. Especially when you put it that way."

"It all depends upon how you perceive the essence of things. And remember I said that essence is energy. Look just above the horizon, at the top the tree line. Take your time and then tell me what you see, Esaugetuh said.

"A wavy line following the shape of the trees as they point skyward. It's a radiating wave," I said.

"Good! In Tibetan Tantrism this is *chaitanya*, meaning radiant consciousness. Oh, sure, some would say it's simply the trees giving off heat from the day's sun. I call it Energy. Listen to the rush of the river. Energy. Listen to the crackle of the fire. Energy. Listen to your own heartbeat. Energy. Everything is energy including the universe itself. It is alive and it is you!" The early Greeks understood the significance of energy. Many of their early myths illustrate that. Do you know the story of Zeus and Semele?"

"I think Semele was one of the many earthlings with whom Zeus had an affair."

"Yes. Hera, Zeus's wife, tricked the poor woman into demanding that Zeus reveal himself to her to prove his divinity. When he did, she was immediately incinerated. Zeus is pure energy and represents that quality throughout the universe."

"Are you saying that energy existed before the material world?" I asked.

"Of course. As I have said, you must first learn to see the essence of the things around you. Then you can see the essence, the energy, of your own Self—the *I* of the *I-Am*. Once you have achieved that you can look at the essence of the universe itself, the noumenon of all experience," Esaugetuh said.

"That's one hell of an assignment. Just how do I go about recognizing this energy?"

"Every living thing on this earth feels energy. Humans have the capacity to sensitize their beings to a higher degree than most other life forms. Notice I said most other life forms, not all," Esaugetuh said, stooping over to put another hunk of wood to our fire.

"That doesn't tell me squat."

"You should feel little shocks of discomfort, not unlike a mild electrical current passing through your body. If you've ever been to a chiropractor and he used a machine to massage an injury you felt a prickly sensation. That's what you should feel when you tune into the energy of the universe. Most people simply equate this feeling to a prickly sensation that goes away. Maybe you'd understand it better if you thought of it as a foot going to sleep and the feeling you have when you move it. When you have those feelings don't ignore them. Tune in. Listen with your whole being. If necessary change your perspective. Once you've caught on, you will feel a sense of warmth flow over your body immediately followed by a cooling. No, not a chill, more like a gentle breeze."

We sat for a while without talking, watching the fire burn itself out. Suddenly Esaugetuh stood up, unzipped his pants, and urinated on the last few burning embers. Turning to me he said, "I'm going to sleep now. You watch the stars."

Esaugetuh sat down, cross-legged and pulled a blanket up around him.

Okay, I thought, since he doesn't want to use the tent, neither will I.

I dragged my sleeping bag out into the open, crawled in, and lay there looking at the stars remembering past times when I had looked at them and wondered. That seemed like a million years ago. Now here I am, like a little kid, spellbound by the heavens above me. And yet a nagging thought continued to intrude: Man can't spend his life looking at the stars. There would be no achievement if he did. And if that's all I do, I'll never find the answers to my questions. Tomorrow I'll ask questions and expect answers.

CHAPTER SEVENTEEN
TWO QUESTIONS

Our perceiving self is nowhere to be found within the world-picture, because it itself is the world-picture.
Erwin Schrödinger

The smell of freshly brewed coffee and sizzling sounds welcomed me to a new morning. The air, crisp, clear, and clean was refreshing as I filled my lungs. The sky was ablaze with a symphony of colors that any artist would envy. I got up, went over to the edge of the sandbar and splashed ice cold water on my face. I stepped behind the tent to relive myself. When I came back around the tent, Esaugetuh handed me a plate of fried fish. I was about to dive in when I realized he was praying. Something I would learn he did before eating. Whatever the language he spoke in, maybe it was a combination of French and his tribal tongue, he kept it short.

We ate in silence. When we were finished I took our plates, scraped them off, and then sloshed them around in the river to complete the cleaning. With the second cup of coffee, Esaugetuh brought out his pipe, filled it, and then lit it with a twig from the fire. He was in no hurry to speak so I opened the conversation.

"Got two questions for you this morning," I said.

"Uh-huh."

"First, what is this body of energy you talk about, this cosmological constant?"

"Again, I remind you to change your perspective. It's not body energy. Body suggests a material being. Another of the Ancients, the Egyptians, claimed that every body had attached to it a double—a light shadow, a mirrored reflection of the human figure, reproduced in minute detail. The Egyptians called this double, *ka*. In short, we are talking about a counterpart of the material form you and I normally call the body. British author, C. S. Lewis talked about *eldil*, a translucent being capable of traveling at great speeds over vast distances. Lewis said that if you attempted to look at one of them it became invisible and the brightness that was there leaves a spot where you had looked. By that I mean, it was somewhere else, thus actually giving the sense of being in two places at once," Esaugetuh said.

"Come on! You've got to be kidding. Okay, I get it. You're talking about Schrödinger's cat. You know very well that something can't be dead and alive at the same time or that something can be in two places at the same time."

"Recently your scientists—,"

"My scientists? What the hell is that supposed to mean?"

"*Non-Native* scientists [15] have demonstrated that an atom can exist in two widely separated places at the same time. A single object, then, can exist in a multiplicity of forms and places. This certainly suggests that such objects can instantly respond to each other's experiences even when they are at opposite ends of the universe. The Ancients knew this eons ago. Is the Egyptian *ka* really any different than Lewis's *eldil*? I think not. Isn't it similar to the idea of the supernatural doppelganger? Your people talk of ghosts and my people talk of *no-man*. Are they not just different metaphors for the same thing?"

A splash in the river broke into our conversation. I caught just a glimpse of an eagle catching its morning breakfast. I marveled at its wing span and the power those wings held. The river, a beautiful green-blue sparkled in the morning sun, hypnotic.

"It's true the human body is composed of energy, but the difference here is that the energy I am speaking about has no mass. Like Zeus, it only has the appearance of mass. This energy can perform acts that are beyond the possibilities of the human physical body. For example, such energy could transport itself instantly from one location to another."

"Is that how you get from one place to another?" I asked.

"Is that your second question?"

"Well no, but I'd like an answer to that one as well," I said.

"I'll pass on that one for now. There's a more important implication in what I've been telling you. The implication is that on the most fundamental level, reality is not divided, that is, it's whole. This becomes even more interesting if we consider that the westerners' division between mind and world is an illusion. There is another basis for such a statement about unity. All of the mystical traditions and beliefs [16] of the world's major religions view reality, spiritual reality, as unified essence. Did you get that? A unified essence. Grasp that and you have gained much in your search for an understanding of the noumenon," Esaugetuh said, sighing.

"Okay, so I listen to what I hear and look at what I see, and accept the notion of the unity of spiritual essence, so what? What does that do for me? I don't see how my understanding of these concepts moves me any closer to the answer to my questions."

"Get rid of that negative attitude. Listen to the song of the universe, withhold judgments, especially those that involve either/or constructs. If you don't, all you will have accomplished in this aspect of your personal journey is a personal negation of the Self. And the end result is a waste of energy and *death* as you would have it called. Whether you are conscious of it or not, you are one with the energy of all that exists and you do not have the right to ignore that which is. Change your perspective. You can vary your experience of the universe, of the physical world, of the energy you see. Look at the river that flows by us. Do you see its water in your mind?" Esaugetuh said.

"Not physically," I replied, put out by his criticism of me.

"Good. Just because you are aware of it doesn't mean the river has wetness in your mind yet you know that it has the quality of wetness as well as speed, coldness, a living substance. Understanding this should be your starting point for your change in perspective. Second, you have to change out of Necessity."

He dragged on his pipe and the smoke spiraled upwards, lazily floating until it melded into the totality of the universe.

"You had a second question?" Esaugetuh asked.

CHAPTER EIGHTEEN
QUESTION TWO: THE PROMETHEAN LEGACY REVEALED

To suffer woes which Hope thinks infinite;
To forgive wrongs darker than death or night;
To defy Power, which seems omnipotent;
To love and bear; to hope till Hope creates
From its own wreck the thing it contemplates;
Neither to change, nor falter, nor repent;
This, like thy glory, Titan, is to be
Good, great and joyous, beautiful and free.
Percy Bysshe Shelly
(Prometheus Unbound)

"You just mentioned *necessity* again. Why necessity?" I asked.

Smoke rings from the old clay pipe billowed and then spiraled upwards, a sure sign he was not happy with my question.

Shit, I thought, now I've pissed him off again.

But to my surprise, he was not.

"Probably the best way to explain the whole idea of *necessity* is with a story of the Ancient Greek God, Prometheus," Esaugetuh said.

"I remember him. He was the fire-thief."

"Well, to begin with, he really wasn't a thief. However, that's not the fundamental issue. This is going to take quite a while so you might as well get comfortable." Esaugetuh said.

"No problem," I replied, pushing my feet a bit closer to the fire. I noticed him looking at me with his blue eyes. I could almost feel him wondering about me. He always seemed to be searching for something he saw in me or wanted to see in me. Most likely it was something he hoped to see, some quality of character.

Damned if I know what it is, I thought as I waited for him to begin.

"Most of the Ancient Greek heroes, while stirring our fantasies and fostering our dreams, often seem out of reach as role models. They're too strong, or too crafty, or too attractive, or too sensual for us ordinary folk to realistically identify with them. However, one among all of those great Greek heroes and deities, was different—Prometheus, the Titan.

He is the creator god, the epitome of the very ideals appropriate to even the most ordinary aspects of our human nature—truth and honor. He shows us the simple things that inexorably link us to other human beings in the greater cosmic chain of existence and in universal experience. In this way, he proves to be an authentic model for all of us."

"What'd he leave us, mankind, if it's not his character as thief?" I asked as I remembered another infamous thief who was freed so others could slay a god.

"You're sure hung up on that thief business. Anyway, Prometheus goes beyond being just a role model of morality."

"What do you mean by that?" I asked, knowing he had me hooked. Just for a moment, I thought I caught a glimmer of a grin on his face. "How can anyone be above a moral model?"

"He is, of course, above all else, a hero. Oh, not in the same sense as Herakles or Odysseus or Hector, the Trojan. You ever read anything by Joseph Campbell?"

"Some of his stuff, sure. Why?"

"Well, in one of his many books [17], Campbell tells us that after facing great tribulation, the hero returns from his quest to the ordinary world bringing gifts to his fellow human beings. Our question now becomes what are these gifts? Campbell suggests that the task of the hero is to teach the lessons he has learned much as the prisoner in Plato's "Allegory of the Cave.""

"So you're saying Prometheus is not a thief, but a hero and that he has to teach us something?" I asked.

"Most assuredly. His adventures in the war of the Titans, his creation of man, his involvement in the Great Flood, his defiance of Zeus by refusing to divulge who will be Zeus' successor, and his crucifixion combine to make him a hero. But there is so much more to Prometheus than his heroism," Esaugetuh replied.

"More than a being a hero? What can be more than that?"

"More than a hero because most heroes are one dimensional whereas, Prometheus is multidimensional. And in this, the Greeks certainly foreshadowed Shakespeare. Furthermore, Prometheus tells us what his gift is when he says, 'blind hopes I lodged within their [humankind's] breasts. [18] And there it is! That something more than just a moral standard. Hope!" Esaugetuh said, his voice breaking with emotion.

"And how'd he give this 'hope' to mankind?"

"Good question," Esaugetuh said.

I couldn't believe my ears. He actually thought I had a good question.

"To begin with, let's look at the trait that is most crucial to his fulfilling the role of hero. In the Promethean mythology, Zeus appears to be the antagonist of the Titan, but this apparent animosity is true only at a surface level. The real antagonist for Prometheus, just as it is for you, is Necessity—that *necessity* that exists within the very structure of the universe. You awake? Paying attention?"

"I am," I said.

"That you are. What I'm telling you will be very important to you later. Always remember *necessity*. It's through his actions that Prometheus shows us the workings of necessity within the cosmic structure thus revealing a universal truth about that web of human existence."

"What was his response; what were his reactions to necessity."

"Well, I can tell you right now, the one thing he did not do was to ride out and slay it as if it were a dragon. He submitted to it!" Esaugetuh said.

"Nothing like giving up. What the hell kind of behavior is that you want me to emulate?"

"Prometheus' posture of submitting to Necessity is not a loss of personhood or dignity by giving up, giving in, or of becoming subservient in a demeaning way. No, this submission represents, instead, the highest degree of spiritual insight and wisdom—to know what is and to live accordingly. And Adam, isn't that one of your concerns?"

"Well, sure. Isn't it everyone's?"

"Notice that Zeus, by contrast, shows us a less noble lifestyle by vaunting a rebellious individualism in ignorance of the truth, that he is a self-willed person living an illusion that he, as a Self, is separate from all other reality. He is pure Ego in the worst sense of the word. I'm sure you can think of any number of famous sports figures, television and movie celebrities that qualify for that description."

"Man, that's one hell of a contrast."

"Yes and that contrast brings to mind two very important concepts that come to us from the East: *Dharma* and *Atman*. Dharma is the universal order of that which is right and just. It expresses itself in a practical way in our social world through our laws and obligations. It's expected that people will live by them. The most moral and upright person is the one who best perceives the Dharma and submits to it. That individual is also the most spiritually enlightened and fulfilled," Esaugetuh said.

"I notice you said, 'best perceives' and that suggests, at least to me, that there are degrees of perceiving Dharma. In other words, some see rightness and justice better than others. If you see Dharma better than I, then does that make you a more enlightened and fulfilled person that me? More upright and just? Doesn't such a notion set up blatant discrimination?

"No. The principle behind dharma is compassion. I'm simply saying that some have arrived while others have yet to arrive. There is no basis for discrimination, as you put it, intended."

"And so we have those who have arrived and those who have not. Then what?"

"That's why there are teachers."

"Hmm. So what about this Atman?" I asked.

"Simply put it means 'self' or 'person' and in this limited sense, it means a person who sees himself as a separate being. In a specific sense, it's the transcending to be one with the Cosmic Reality. Dharma and Atman are two very fundamental Hindu concepts and are connected in an affirmation that human suffering is released by dispelling the ignorance about the self and by submitting to that which is universal."

"So you're saying Zeus was ignorant about the Self?"

"Yes. Just as you are," Esaugetuh said, pulling on his pipe.

"You nuts? You've got to be kidding. I'm not like Zeus."

"Ah, but you are! And I'll get back to that issue with you, but right now I want to continue with Prometheus. If you're still up for it."

"If there's coffee left, you want some?" I asked.

I poured out two cups of coffee and sat the pot off the fire. Since I was squatted by the fire I added some more small broken branches. It flared for a moment, settled itself, and behaved as it should. The rocks around the fire pit maintained their heat. It felt good.

"Hand me your cup. A bit of brandy will warm your gut," Esaugetuh said, stretching out his hand to take my cup. Continuing he said, "Prometheus gives us hope based on a faith-assumption, that is, that Necessity is good, not malicious or capricious. Our highest good is found in submitting to Necessity. And this is not that much different than submitting to Dharma."

"Explain," I said, smarting a little under the implied criticism.

"Prometheus' name is related to our word 'promise.' In Latin, *promissa* means to send forth and when combined with the Greek word —*theos* meaning 'god,' we find that the name Prometheus means *the god who sends forth*. In a religious sense 'promise' can also mean 'divine assurance.' Prometheus' divine assurance or benediction is the hope that Necessity need not be an adversary, thus providing motivation for human survival and giving us a sense of well-being," Esaugetuh said, as smoke rings floated lazily up from his pipe.

"So how does that connect Necessity, Dharma, and Prometheus?"

"Well, well. There might be hope for you yet," Esaugetuh said, leaning over and gently slapping me on the back of my head. "Necessity is equivalent to the Greek, *logos,* Universal Reasoning. In Greek Philosophy, we are told that *logos* is what underlies and governs the universe. See any connection with Dharma?"

"Sure."

"Good. The Stoics, especially, used this idea. It's interesting to note that John, The Christian evangelist, was so bold as to assert that 'Logos became flesh and made his dwelling among us,' a reference to Jesus Christ. Without this affirmation that Necessity is on our side, what hope do we have? What hope do you have?" Esaugetuh said, sipping his coffee.

"Look," I said, "I'll accept your word that Prometheus is a role model of this truth you're talking about, but a lot of people are truthful, but that fact doesn't make them heroes. Earlier you said I should follow my bliss when you were quoting Joseph Campbell. That my bliss was my truth. So if each of us has our own truth, how do we know which is *the truth*?" Do we have the right to insist that others follow what we have determined as being the truth?"

"You're struggling with a semantic issue. You are talking about truth as in, to tell the truth as opposed to lying. I am talking about that which is, always has been, and always will be, that which is the ground of existence. Your bliss and how you define it is your ground of being simply because it is that which identifies you as a Self.

Prometheus, besides being a role model of this truth, is a teacher—a teacher to us as well as to the old gods themselves. In the Old Literature, he even dares to teach Zeus those necessary lessons for enlightened governance, thus ensuring Zeus' survival. Even though this action of kindness toward Zeus would seem incompatible with the conflict between them, it is important to remember that the Promethean struggle was not with Zeus, but with Necessity. This struggle involves the Promethean belief system."

"Whew! Are you saying that this Promethean belief system is of a higher moral order that he appeals to and by implication, so should I?"

"Uh huh. His whole story implies a higher moral order. There are two specific charges that question Prometheus' moral fiber and consequently his authenticity as a hero, as a role model, and as a teacher. I have to ask is he a thief and a trickster as so many interpreters of his story have stated. If such charges are true how can I uphold him as a character of truth and honor, one for you to emulate? Can I justify calling him a hero? Dare I propose him as an ideal universal role model? And finally, can you accept him as a prophet of understanding, as an example of how to deal with Necessity?

Admittedly, the charges have some substance but only superficially. The ancient literature strongly suggests that Prometheus did seek and obtain permission from Zeus to lessen the burdensome sacrifice expected from the humans. This intervention allowed the humans to keep a portion of the animal sacrifice for themselves. It's true that he returned the fire to the mortals but it should not seriously be viewed as a theft since he was returning that gift from Zeus, to begin with. One doesn't give a gift and then take it back. His courage, integrity, and honor show that you can, without reservation, affirm him as a heroic model. He is above all else, a person of principle."

"Wasn't he nailed to the cross, so to speak?" I asked.

"Yes. For his courage and integrity, Prometheus suffered the humiliating *apotumpanismos*, a form of public execution, during which the condemned who is stripped naked, is nailed by spikes to a pole erected in the ground. [19] In Prometheus' case, he was chained to a large rock and had his side pierced. He was chained on Mt. Caucasus,

'an uninhabited waste at the world's end.' [20]

"What could possibly motivate Prometheus to suffer such a crucifixion? By the way, wasn't there a liver-eating bird involved and endless days and nights of heat and cold?" I asked.

"Again I'll repeat myself," Esaugetuh said as smoke billowed up from his clay pipe. "It's his commitment to his belief system. Your question, however, should have been what is his belief system? You still haven't learned to ask the right questions. Better feed the fire. The temperature is dropping."

I put more wood on the fire. I stirred it up a bit causing sparks to fly up into the air.

He just can't avoid giving me a dig, I thought as I watched the sparks fly.

"Prometheus believes that he has an obligation to that which he holds most dear, his creation. Reach over there in that bag," Esaugetuh said, pointing to a backpack. "There's some jerky in it. It's going to be a long night. You'll probably need to have something to eat."

"Obligation? What obligation is he under?" I said, handing him the dried meat.

"He created man, taught him arts and crafts as well as how to make sacrifice to the gods, and how to keep a fire. All of this indicates his sense of duty rooted in love. His decision to side with Zeus during the Titanomachian conflict and to help install Zeus on the throne reinforces his sense of obligation. He went to the aid of Zeus because his brother Titans committed themselves to physical force. When Zeus exhibited unbridled and raw misuse of power, Prometheus acted. He felt an obligation to teach Zeus how to be more compassionate. Because of his love, Prometheus risked the vengeance of the gods to keep human beings alive. He shows his love for Zeus when he acts as Zeus' midwife in the birthing of Athena. Perhaps nothing shows Prometheus' belief system more eloquently than his statement, 'When Zeus no longer knows his mind, or can see his hand, he will reach for me. And I—what can I do but welcome him?'" [21]

"Man, that's something else. He's quite a character. Most I remember about him from mythology is that he stole fire and Zeus nailed his ass for it," I said, tearing into a piece of dried meat.

"Prometheus continued to reveal the nature of his fundamental beliefs when he simply said, 'I sought mercy to give mortals preference.' That comment shows the real nature of the Promethean will: the nature of the intent of the action determines its morality. That is, all value lies only in the intention, an approach to morality Immanuel Kant espoused several centuries later. His, 'I sought mercy . . .' designates the intent as *good will*."

A loud splash and heavy breathing interrupted Esaugetuh. I thought we were about to be invaded by Big-Foot or some other monstrous creature. Sensing my apprehension Esaugetuh said, "Nothing to worry about. Elk. About four or five of them. Crossing the river."

CHAPTER NINETEEN
THE HUNTER

The flow of the present experience is the only libation that can quench the thirsty soul.
John David Birch
(Flux and Flow)

Rising before dawn to ready himself for the hunt, Esaugetuh was mindful of his clothing, deerskin head to foot. His moccasins contained no fancy bead-work or tassels, not any of that kind of silly stuff you find in the shops. Leather tongs held them on his feet. A fixed blade hunting knife housed it its leather sheath and a hatchet were tucked into a leather sash tied around his waist. Hesitating for a moment, he pulled the stag horn knife from its sheath, thumbed its blade. Satisfied as to its sharpness he put it back into its sheath and repeated the process with the hatchet. Next, he picked up a small leather bag, slung its strap over his head and let it hang down his left side. It contained two pieces of jerky and a hard biscuit. It had been quite some time since he had been on a hunt. He hoped he hadn't lost his touch.

He eased the skiff into the water and let its swift moving current take him down stream. As he floated along, giving the skiff a nudge with a paddle to keep it centered he enjoyed the early morning view. It quenched his thirsty soul, a libation much needed to energize his spiritual being. Dawn slowly raised her nightshade so all who were watching could see her splendor. And there were watching eyes other than those belonging to Esaugetuh.

Sunrise was like an elegant woman dressed in pink hues splashed against a token of sapphire blue. Golden streaks slowly followed her as she floated across the sky. The ice-white jewels standing as guardians of the valley formed a necklace and reflected the exquisite colors of her morning gown. He noticed a bald eagle soaring high up along the mountain rim.

For a moment he thought of past times, imagining he was in a birch canoe, listening to the tong-tong drums announcing his movement along the river on his way to an Indian village. It wasn't that he wished for that life again.

No, he thought. Just a romantic notion. Those days were not less burdened than these of this time. The trials and tribulations weren't really all that different. People still struggle to survive, have hopes, dreams, fears, and sorrows. And now I have a new challenge, young Adam.

He smiled at the thought of Adam.

Coming to a spot he liked, Esaugetuh eased the skiff toward the bank, dragged it up from the water, and fastened it to a tree and shadow-like he entered the woods, disappearing into its bowels. He jogged along at an easy pace. He was in no hurry as he relished each new smell the forest offered up to him. The raucous call of the ever- watchful crow announced his presence in the woods. For a short time, it followed him, literally hopping from limb to limb from one tree to another. Just as suddenly it flew away, back toward where it first picked up Esaugetuh. It either sensed no danger or it tired of the chase. Esaugetuh was glad for the quiet; he didn't need a squawking bird to tip off the elk. He moved close to the evergreen trees, letting their boughs rub against him, camouflaging his scent. He slowed his pace, scanning the woods as he walked along.

Finally, deep in the woods, he found what he was looking for, a yew tree. Cautiously he looked around. There still remained an unease haunting him from a dream he had in which he saw dark shadows. He considered it a bad sign. The single crow was a bad sign. A shudder ran through him.

Quickly he cut a branch from the yew tree, cleared it of its leaves, notched the ends, pulled a piece of deer tendon from his jacket and used it to string the bow. His movements were so quiet, so smooth not one leaf moved on the yew tree when he cut it. Moving on, he next looked for Arrow-wood, [22] found it, cut a shaft for one arrow. One was enough. After fletching it, testing it for balance, and finally satisfied as to its strength, Esaugetuh was ready for the kill.

He took off at a swift trot, taking care not to make noise. He soon picked up fresh tracks, four cows, and one bull, not that uncommon because of the weather. A few miles further, deep in a lodgepole pine thicket, he found them grazing. He shook off a chill. Stopped. Looked around. His keen eyes searching for a sign. He listened. Nothing. Yet he knew it was there, stalking him as he stalked the elk. Being careful not to be seen, or heard,

Esaugetuh stayed downwind of the animals. Cautiously he maneuvered himself to within a hundred yards. Still too far away for a good shot. Esaugetuh decided that he would have to tease the bull into coming closer.

Esaugetuh gave a cow-call, soft and low. He knew he had to convince the bull that one of his cows was wandering off. The bull bugled back and moved toward Esaugetuh. As experienced as he was, Esaugetuh always felt his spine tingle when he heard that sound. Next Esaugetuh squealed like a young bull; followed that with a series of short high-pitched grunts. The bull wheeled around and stood broadside to Esaugetuh giving him a perfect shot, just behind the shoulder.

Slowly and in a single rhythmic stroke, Esaugetuh pulled back on his bow. The arrow quickly found its mark and the Wapiti [23] bolted. It ran a couple hundred yards and dropped. It was easy for Esaugetuh to follow its trail. Cautiously he approached the downed animal. If it were not dead, it could thrash out and its sharp hooves could be deadly. He watched its chest cavity. It was not moving.

Esaugetuh made short work dressing the elk out, cutting off enough fresh meat for Adam and his needs. He strung the rest high up in a tree to keep it from predators. Scratching around on the ground, Esaugetuh found seven small stones, piled them at the base of the tree and then lay in a forked tree branch, pointing north. With the meat slung over his broad shoulders, Esaugetuh headed back to the skiff. He moved as a young man, sure-footed, purposeful and inwardly pleased with his day's work.

He felt good. There was hope for a new day, a new beginning. He felt it deep within his soul.

No, it goes deeper than my soul. Much deeper. It goes as deep as the universe itself, he thought as he trotted along.

Adam's hope. He doesn't know it yet. I've got so much to tell him, so much to teach him.

An inner voice cautioned: Teach him now; tell him later.

Paddling upstream, against the swift current of the Skagit, was not possible. He pulled the skiff further upon the river's bank, deflated it, rolled it up, tied it, and slung it over his back. He would have to walk back up river, inflate the skiff again, and float back down stream to the sandbar. Fortunately, the small pump that was part of the skiff was battery operated.

Got to give Adam credit for that one, he thought as he trudged along.

He stopped several times to listen, to look. He was sure he caught a shadow moving north with him. Whatever it was, even in his dreams, it was always a shadowy thing, nothing well defined. His instincts told him it was bad. Maybe it was Death stalking him. He knew he was old. Had he not heard the hoot of an owl?

Maybe, he thought, I should have cut another arrow.

He knew he should soon be nearing the sandbar where they were camped. He hadn't realized he had gone down stream quite so far. He decided to stop and rest. He pulled a piece of jerky from his pouch, slowly chewed it, letting his saliva moisten it. And while he rested and chewed on the jerky Adam was awakened by the high-pitched whistle of an eagle.

Slowly Adam sat up in his sleeping bag, rubbed his eyes, not believing what he saw. The eagle was sitting just a few feet away; it looked directly at Adam, opened its mouth as if to speak. Adam sat, frozen and barely breathing, mesmerized by the splendor of the huge bird. It unfolded its large wings, gave a little jump, and took off.

"My god. Esaugetuh did you see that? Did you see that?" I yelled, scrambling to get out of my sleeping bag.

I was so excited I didn't even notice the beautiful morning. I poked my head into the pop-up tent. No Esaugetuh. As I turned around, I noticed the skiff was gone.

"That son-of-a-bitch! He's gone and left me, stranded on this god-damned sandbar and no way to get back across the river," I said out loud.

I picked up my backpack and felt around inside to make sure my gun was still there. It was. I decided to make some coffee. It was near the fire pit that I found his note saying he had gone hunting and would be back in time for breakfast.

Well at least he left a note this time, I thought, remembering all too well his past disappearances.

After having been on the river for nearly three days I really felt the need of a bath. Even though the river was icy cold, I pulled off my clothes and jumped in, feet first. For a moment I thought I was going to die. The shock and pain were unbelievable.

The current was swift and I was being dragged down stream. Panic almost got me. I started swimming, stroke after hard stroke. I struggled to get back upon the bank, sucking in air, shaking, barely able to stand. I stumbled around, found a blanket, wrapped myself in it, and bent down to the fire pit. I gathered up some of the shavings Esaugetuh had made, put a few small pieces of dry twigs on top. I remembered I had three matches. One worked and I had a small fire. Carefully I nursed it into being, added some more wood. Esaugetuh had replenished our fuel supply. I put the pot on to warm the coffee left over from the night before.

I got the bottle of brandy and poured a hefty shot into my cup. I got up, brought my clothes closer to the fire to get them warm. Once I had calmed down and had stopped my shaking I thought about Esaugetuh. I knew he was old and the river might be too much for him to navigate. Then it occurred to me that I didn't know how he was going to kill anything. He had no gun.

"Damn! Maybe the note is just a ruse. Maybe he really has left me out here," I muttered.

My stomach told me it was badly in need of food. I grabbed the bag that had the jerky in it. Ravenously I chewed on a hunk. Suddenly I stopped chewing.

What if this is all there is? Better conserve, I thought, putting the remainder of the meat back. This is ridiculous. Of course, he'll be back. Why wouldn't he? What was it he said? 'Change your perspective and your perception will change.' Yeah, that was it was. Okay, get some more wood for the fire, keep it going. Put some wet grass on it so it will smoke. Esaugetuh will see that.

I began to watch the river for any sign of him. All kinds of ugly thoughts ballooned and then popped in and out of my brain as I paced up and down, straining to see some dark object floating my way. Maybe he had a heart attack, maybe a wild animal got him, maybe the skiff overturned and he had drowned. Thoughts like that. The sun was nearing high noon and still no sign of Esaugetuh. I actually thought of firing my gun to try and attract the attention of passing vehicles. I knew they couldn't see me, the sandbar being around a bend in the river and out of view of the road. I thought they might hear the shot. I dismissed that as sheer stupidity.

Good god, no wonder Esaugetuh thinks I'm dumb, I thought.

Finally, I stopped my pacing and stood, statue-like wrapped in my blanket, watching the river. Then I spotted him. He was too far way to tell if he had anything in the skiff with him. Yet I sensed he had been successful. He was sitting straight-backed with his head erect. He was the picture-perfect hunter returning with his kill, bringing much needed food back to the family.

Family? Man, I've not thought about my parents in months. Wonder if they have thought of me.

CHAPTER TWENTY
THE PROMETHEAN WILL

Feelings characterize the person in whom they appear, the person who experiences them.
Georg Kühlewind
(The Life of the Soul)

I was so glad to see him that I grabbed him and gave him a bear hug. My blanket fell to the ground. And there I was bare-assed naked for the whole world to see.

"Better get some clothes on, show off," Esaugetuh said, laughing.

"What's with the laughing?" I said, standing there shivering.

"Someday you'll make good babies," Esaugetuh replied.

And that embarrassed me even more. It didn't take long for me to get my clothes on. Their warmth felt good next to my cold skin.

"Went for a swim. Guess you forgot to take your clothes off. Bad idea, swimming here. River's dangerous," Esaugetuh said as he poked the fire back to life.

"No, I didn't leave my clothes on. And you're right about the river. Man, it's moving. You ever wonder where it's rushing off to."

"Uh huh. We'll have some elk, Esaugetuh said as he returned to the skiff.

He retrieved several bunches of plants. As he handed me a sample from each bunch he instructed me to smell each, to note the leaf and stem structure, and to put each to my tongue.

"If it's really bitter or if it gives a slight stinging sensation to the tongue, don't eat it. The first one I gave you is a leak. Notice the long leaf, the shade of green, feel the edge of the leaf. They're cultivated now but the wild ones are much better in taste. These are wild peas. Notice the smallness of the leaves, the yellow pods. They have a sweet taste as well as smell. Now here's one for you. Your mother probably grew this in her flower bed. It's carrot or Queen Anne's Lace. Pay attention to the way the top branches out. The last is a tuber. It has the texture and color of a potato, but it is long rather than round.

He wrapped them together in their wet leaves and placed them along the edge of the fire. They'll steam nicely," Esaugetuh said as he cut a large slice of elk into two steaks.

"Why didn't you take me with you? I thought you were going to teach me Indian ways and certainly hunting is one of them." I said.

"No. My task, if you want to call it that, is not to make you an Indian. It wouldn't work."

"Why? Why not?"

"We're of different worlds, you and I. You're—,"

"But weren't you going to make me your successor? Isn't that why you adopted me?"

"Yes and I did, but you can't be what you are not. We live in different worlds. Yet, there is a dimension in which both of us can exist. My hope is that I can teach you how to live and survive in both dimensions," Esaugetuh said, turning the elk steaks.

"Don't give me that Don Juan [24] shit. I know damn well what's real and what's not. Different dimensions? That's a crock."

"I didn't say I wasn't real. Here," he said, handing me his knife "cut me. See if I don't bleed."

"Okay. I surrender," I said, shaking my head.

"For a minute, think about the lessons you've learned today. Think carefully," Esaugetuh said, raising one eyebrow as he looked at me.

"Well, for one thing, I learned to be more careful in choosing my swimming hole. I did remember to jump in feet first."

"Anything else?"

"Yeah, I learned that I can trust you," I said.

"Trust me?"

"Yes. I really don't know you. You could have slit my throat at any time with that awesome knife of yours. You could have left me stranded on this sandbar."

"Okay. What else?"

"Well, I've learned what wild plants I can eat. Speaking of eating, that steak ready yet?"

It was. I gorged myself. The flavors were sharp and distinct and the meat was tender. Best meal I'd had in a long time. Esaugetuh had really outdone himself with this one.

"Yesterday, you were telling me about the idea of intent and good-will. Care to elaborate?"

"Sure. I was actually talking about Immanuel Kant, the German philosopher. He's one of my favorites. For him, as it is for me, the moral worth of an action or behavior is determined by the principle the individual follows. A man with goodwill does things out of respect for the moral law."

"But what is the moral law in the story of Prometheus? What does the morality of Olympian rule require, or for that matter, permit? Wasn't Zeus a usurper of the throne? And if so, does one have to adhere to the moral law of such a usurper? Seems to me that we've had our share of despots, dictators, or tyrants recently."

"Well, glad to see you're beginning to get the hang of the type of question to ask. Applying the Kantian principle, we find that Prometheus believes that a person, in this case, a god named Zeus, ought to treat others with fairness and justice. Zeus, on the other hand, believes that force will get him what he wants. Prometheus believes one ought to share with those less fortunate; Zeus believes it is his right to exploit others. Thus, when Prometheus states he sought in mercy, the conflict between the two moral systems reveals itself. Unfortunately, it is not sufficiently resolved."

"What you're saying is that there's a duality at play, one personified by Prometheus, the other by Zeus," I said, enjoying the conversation.

"Yes. Prometheus, the model of love, honor, friendship, and correct social instincts pits himself against the tyranny and cruelty of Zeus. Yet, I don't paint Prometheus as light and Zeus as dark—the one as white and other as black or as personifications of good and evil. That would belie the intent of the ritual of the 'new learning from the old.' That the business we are about, isn't it? You and me?"

"Yes. I'm trying to learn from you. Even though I don't see what we're doing has anything to do with being a shaman."

"All in good time. All in good time. You have to understand that the mind of Zeus is not open to reason. The conflict between the two focuses and it's not oedipal nor is it lust. Instead, it concerns itself with the education of a *closed mind.*"

"Now you just wait a damn minute. Are you telling me I have a closed-mind? That's not fair. And you know it's not," I yelled at him.

"Grow up!" Esaugetuh snapped. "You need to learn that not every remark is pointed at you. Get over this self-sensitivity. Nearly lost my thought because of your interruption. I was about to say the education of a closed mind with the Promethean ideals of fairness, justice tempered with compassion, and love. What will be will be. What is, is by Necessity. He has no choice but to teach Zeus.

The Promethean approach to Necessity is distinct. Prometheus' whole being, his total existence functions out of Necessity. As 'seer,' Prometheus has foreknowledge of events to come: he reveals to Io her destiny, he knows which female will birth a son that will surpass the father, he knows of the great flood Zeus intends to use to destroy humankind, and he knows that Zeus will set him free from his chains. These glimpses into the future bring about certain Promethean actions. Prometheus participates with Necessity, whereas, humans tend toward tenacity for fighting it, evidence of a lesson not yet learned. The Greeks knew where it was at. Too bad we got so caught up with Socrates, Plato, and Aristotle and forgot the lessons of their myths."

"And my unlearned lesson?" I asked, looking at the fire, not wanting him to see the tears.

If he intended to hurt me he was successful. Even my own father never treated me with such a personal reproach. For a moment, a flashing moment, I actually thought of getting up, getting in the skiff and leaving him on the sand bar. Maybe he had a lesson to learn. I was in such a deep pout I almost didn't hear what he said.

"Better make that lessons, not lesson."

There it was again. Another dig. What the hell am I doing out here in the middle of a god-damned river with an old geezer? I'm nuts. I'm not getting any input on Native medicines and healing. That was the reason for my tracking him down. No! That's a lie. That was the excuse I created to justify my search. Man, what a piece of work I am. His voice brought my attention back.

"Within Promethean behavior, beliefs and values is a blueprint for dealing with Necessity," Esaugetuh said. "Enough talk. I have a visitor."

With that, I was dismissed. It was obvious that Esaugetuh was expecting him. Squatting by the fire pit, they remained huddled in whispered conversation. And since I wasn't introduced or invited to participate in the talk. Rudeness personified, I thought, as I turned to other things to amuse myself.

The emerald green of the Skagit sparked in the afternoon sun. As it splashed against rocks and fallen trees it jettisoned diamond-white foam into the air. Its beat was the heart-rhythm of the universe. And as water is prone to do, it cast its spell. Ducks and some other waterfowl busied themselves as they bobbed up and down in the swiftly moving water. Once I thought I saw a salmon swim by. It was a piece of wood. Like a kid looking for treasure, I walked along kicking up the sand. I realized I was looking at tracks made the night before by the elk crossing. As I squatted down to take a closer look I caught the sight of a bald eagle swooping down from its perch on a tree. With magical ease, it caught a salmon and flew off to enjoy its meal. I wasn't aware of time passing but the night sky had begun to seek his mate and had begun to spread himself over her. A few remnants of bright colored ribbons effortlessly floated toward the western horizon. My whole being gulped in the sight and I felt so terribly insignificant, so terribly small. Then I felt his hand on my shoulder. There was no need for words.

CHAPTER TWENTY ONE
BLUEPRINT FOR DEALING WITH NECESSITY

You must constantly nourish openness, breadth of vision, willingness, enthusiasm, and reverence; that will change the whole atmosphere of your mind.
Sogyal Rinpoche

"My brother, Long Walker, needed meat for his family. I left him the bulk of the elk. He had walked a great distance. You look surprised." Esaugetuh said.

"Well, yeah. In today's world, I didn't realize people still depended on the hunt."

"There are still some who care for their families in the old way. It was early this morning that I saw his tracks in the deep woods and left him a sign that he would be welcome in our camp. He was not anxious to stay longer."

"Yet he stayed nearly three hours. That doesn't sound anxious to me," I said.

"Ah, wondering why the adopted son of the shaman was not introduced are you." Esaugetuh's laughter came up from deep gut and spilled out into the quickening night.

"The thought occurred to me a few dozen times. I almost joined in and then didn't," I replied.

"Glad you didn't. It would have embarrassed him. He is a good man. Come it's time to get the fire going. How many matches do you have left?"

"Two. I used one earlier. I've not replaced it from the supplies."

"Be sure you do. Always keep the matches dry. I'll show you how to start a fire the old way. You ever in the Boys Scouts?"

"Yeah, but we had a special kit provided by the Scouts. A small block, a pencil-like piece of wood, and a string. We had to find our own dry tinder."

"No kits here. And no string. And another thing, it might be a good idea to carry a couple of fire sticks in your backpack and some dry tinder. In the deep woods, you want to select your location for the fire pit with care. Depending on the weather you could lose your fire from snow, rain. Here, we are fortunate that there is no rain because there's no shelter for the fire."

Effortlessly Esaugetuh had a fire going. He had brought fire sticks with him. He didn't seem in any hurry to have our evening meal. We sat by the fire, watching its flames lick the night air. He indicated that I should sit across from him so I moved. I noticed that he sprinkled some of his tobacco on the fire. After that, he threw a handful of something else on the fire and it immediately blazed. I thought this was done to add a pleasant smell to the fire. I was wrong.

We sat in silence serenaded by a cacophony of sounds. Each new wave moved to a crescendo punctuated with a sudden lack of sound. Dramatic. Who needed a night with Beethoven? As I looked at

Esaugetuh, seated straight-backed, opposite of me I seemed to lose focus, his features became blurred. Everything began to spin around. I sensed something in my hand. It was a cup. I tipped it to my lips and swallowed. Bitterness was followed by an uncontrollable shudder. Quiet stillness. All memory a faint echo from some distant star.

Esaugetuh had my arm and hand, holding them in an iron grip. I saw the flash of his hunting knife and felt the searing pain as he—.

My god, he's killing me, I thought.

I felt him hold me up, holding my hand over the flames. My blood dripped into the fire. It hungrily sought my life's flow. I was dying. Somewhere off in the far, far distance in another time, I heard the beat of the tong-tong drums. Slowly I opened my eyes and saw half naked men dancing in a circle, chanting. Some wore feathers in their hair, others carried gourd rattles. All had their faces painted in reds, blacks, and yellows. One had his face painted white with large black circles painted around his eyes. I tried looking into his eyes. I saw nothing. Suddenly I realized I was in the middle of that circle of dancers, flat on my back. As I raised my head to get a better look I discovered I was covered with wet mud and leaves. What a stinking putrid smell.

As I was about to shout, yell, or scream I felt myself being lifted up into the air. The dancers had me, held me close to the fire, and then they began to pass me over the flames, from one dancer to another. As they lowered me closer to the burning coals with each pass, I felt the heat, the drying of the mud on my skin and as the leaves curled they popped into small little flames.

They are roasting me—alive!

The drums stopped!

The putrid smell of my mud-caked body changed. His voice, light years away, and new tantalizing smells slowly penetrated by consciousness.

"You okay? You were doing an awful lot of moaning."

"Uh, sure. Guess I was dreaming," I said, checking to make sure I wasn't covered in mud and leaves. "What's that smell?"

"Elk meat wrapped in soaked nettles. I brought some nettles back with me from the hunt. I've made some stinging nettles tea for you. Flattened quamash [25] is baking under the hot rocks. Smells good. Nice and sweet."

"Stinging Nettles tea? Man, you've got to be kidding."

"No, I'm not. It helps build your deep energy that's needed to lengthen your life expectancy. Lots of good minerals in it."

"I think my mother used to give that to me when I was in Canada," I said as I carefully looked at my hand. There was a small round dark spot in the middle of my palm. I brushed it off. Mud! It was then that I noticed a small slit about two inches above my right wrist. It appeared to be already healed.

What the hell is going on? I thought.

The sizzle from the cooking meat changed the melody of the night sounds and added a new smell and that changed my thoughts. I was hungry. A starving kind of hunger. And that bothered me. It hadn't been that many hours ago that we had a big lunch. Esaugetuh was watching me even though he appeared to be busy with something on the fire. I felt those penetrating eyes, searching my soul, digging deep. I just wish I knew what he was looking for. His baritone voice finally penetrated the denizens of my brain.

"It's Prometheus' behavior, his belief system, and values that provide a blueprint for dealing with Necessity. The blueprint is there for everyone to see if they would just open their eyes, change their perspective. That's all this is needed. It even foreshadows Buddha-thinking."

There he was again, just picking up as if we had been talking right along. I wonder if he thinks I take notes. Actually, that's what I should be doing.

"Prometheus doesn't use force when he responds to Necessity. He does not struggle against it. He *accepts* it as part of the reality he experiences. Acceptance, not surrender, is the lesson. That's the real message Prometheus brings to mankind. Move with Necessity. By doing so, it allows you to exert your influence, to bring about the changes needed for your survival and to bring about those changes required for humanity's survival. Take our skiff, for example. You let it flow with the river, giving direction only as necessary to keep from smashing against the rocks. The rocks along the river are no different from experiences in life. Each has the potential of danger as well as safety—each has the potential of greatness or infamy—each has the potential for happiness or sorrow. We intercede in the rivulets of life's experiences. In the myth, it is Prometheus who intercedes for mankind and what an intercession it is! Is he not the predecessor of yet another god, who like him, was crucified? What price will the next new god have to pay?" Esaugetuh said.

Whew! The overwhelming implications of what he said has created, no, forged even more questions. I was so engrossed in trying to understand all that he had said and what I had experienced earlier that I didn't even notice that he was sitting directly in front of me. Okay, so there's a blueprint for dealing with Necessity: Go with the flow, don't use force, and give direction. A new god? Is that what this is all about? A new god defined in modern technological terms? Is that the new battle ground? Is that why we are so unhappy. The new god, science, isn't giving us stability. It's always in a state of flux.

I shook my head in rejection. There has to be something more! I looked at Esaugetuh and tried to focus. He was smoking his pipe. The traditional smoke rings floated lazily upward and disappeared. He was content, self-confident, self-assured. He knew exactly who he was.

Damn, I thought, I wish I could be like that, but I'm not.

"Are you okay?" Esaugetuh asked.

"Not sure. A while back I had the darndest dream. Sort of shook me up," I replied.

"Dreams are powerful messengers. You want to tell me about your dream? When did you have it? Last night?"

"No, right here, right now. It was so real. You had just finished showing me how to build a fire. And suddenly I was being passed over a bed of hot coals by a group of half-naked Indians."

"Hmm! So the transformation begins," Esaugetuh said.

For some reason, I didn't pick up on that comment. I guess I was still too preoccupied with how I was going to synthesize all of this. How am I to make it all cohere? What's the metaphor? Don't we learn the metaphors so that we can travel to the depths of our souls? To commune with the gods themselves? For what damnable purpose? To discover ourselves, to learn who we are?

So, what was it that Prometheus accomplished by his antagonizing opposition to the great Zeus? To act out of Necessity is an act of will. By exerting an act of will, Prometheus succeeded in establishing his own individuation, his own meaning. He found his connection to the universal. And because he did, Zeus couldn't kill him. He was eternal. Isn't that what we humans are all trying so desperately to do? To connect? Isn't' that what I am trying to do, this *I of me*? Making that connection identifies who the *I-am* is.

CHAPTER TWENTY TWO
UNIVERSAL CONNECTIVITY

In appearance I'm a thing moving about in space.
In reality I'm that unmoving space itself.
Douglas Harding

"Esaugetuh," I said, "Doesn't the effort to bring about a universal connectivity involve the ego? What I mean, isn't it a creation of the ego in order to make itself important? That's not a good thing, is it?"

"First of all," Esaugetuh began, "Don't be in such a rush to condemn the ego. I know that nearly everything you read nowadays is an outright condemnation of the ego. Probably it's always been that way, at least since it was identified. And that's unfortunate. I think the issue is created by confusion over the actual role of the ego."

"Confusion over its role?"

"Let me come back to that a bit later. For now, just keep in mind, that the ego has a role to play. When considering universal connectivity another word comes to mind that seems to have more relevance."

"More relevance? What's the word?"

"Quintessence. In times past, quintessence was thought as the fifth and highest essence after the four basic elements of earth, fire, water, and air."

"That's one on me. Never heard of it."

"It was thought to be the substance of the heavenly bodies and latent in all things. Actually, very similar to the ancient Egyptian's concept of the SA which was a fluid-like substance that flowed throughout the bodies of their gods. When it came to health, vigor, and all the other necessary life forces. The natives of the Malaysian Archipelago believed in Mana, a life force that existed in all things and afforded connectivity to all things. You know what a Leyden Jar is?"

"Had something to do with electricity, I think."

"Yes. Electricity gathered in a Leyden Jar is fluid and all pervasive. And here I have to be careful in choosing my words, inadequate as they are, they are all we have. I don't want you to misunderstand. Be patient with what I say," Esaugetuh said.

"Okay. Shoot."

"Modern man is just now beginning to open the door to a whole new universe, one not composed of the usual light waves, but one that is non-physical and one that is beyond the usual understanding of space-time. We have been taught that there is nothing faster than the speed of light and for most humans that is sufficient. However, for some, it is not. Because it is not, there is actually developing a theory which includes a concept of speed faster than light. Science fiction genres have had warped speeds, time travel, and quasi-religious themes for quite some time. In relation to quintessential connectivity, they are lack luster. Even the legendary comic book and movie hero, Superman, would not be able to travel at the speed I am now talking about."

"You—,"

I never got to make my comment. From behind us came the most hideous growl imaginable. I had never heard anything like it, not even in the horror movies. Esaugetuh's speech stopped in mid-air. A terrible ripping filled the air. Our tent flew by my head. I looked up, straining to see beyond our fire light. I could detect a massive dark form. Had I been taken back in time again? I tried to determine what the hell was happening. It stepped closer into the light of our camp fire. I saw it then. A monstrous grizzly bear from out of the deep woods. The silver-tipped hair on its huge back and broad shoulders glistened in our firelight. It towered above me, dwarfing my six-foot plus frame, swaying back and forth, saliva dripping from its huge yellowed teeth. I felt the whoosh of air pass my face as its giant flat paws with their long razor-sharp claws swung back and forth. My stomach flip-flopped several times and then I spewed my insides upon the ground. Either my vomiting noise or my vomit caught the bear's attention.

"Don't move," Esaugetuh ordered.

Move? My god! I was absolutely paralyzed. I had my Glock 31 but it was in my backpack which was too damn close to that monster. I thought of trying to inch my way closer but then I saw an even stranger phenomenon. Esaugetuh was dancing, circling the giant bear, always just out of reach of its deadly paws. As it swirled to strike out at Esaugetuh I saw its glazed eyes glowing in the firelight. It was unreal, strange, and illusionary. As Esaugetuh circled the raging bear he seemed to grow taller and taller until he towered about this enormous animal.

I caught sight of my backpack, made a grab for it, pulled out my gun and shoved a shell into its chamber. I waited for the right moment. I didn't have a change to get a shot off. Esaugetuh suddenly threw his arms up into the air, each coming from close to his chest, crossing and ending with the palms of his hands facing the crazed animal. The behemoth stopped, teetered for a brief moment, and then stood very still. Esaugetuh was in my way.

Damn!

Its head burst into an explosion of blue flames. The smell of burnt hair and flesh filled the air and once again it was necessary for me to empty my churning gut. What a mess. The bear's roar was so loud I was sure it would cause an avalanche on Mount Baker several miles away. Then it turned and dove into the Skagit. Its thrashing smothered the sounds of the river itself. Then all was quiet!

I shook my head, trying to clear my mind and that was a big mistake. The waves of nausea flooded me once again. I went down on my knees as the spasms rippled one after the other. I was sure my intestines would be coming up next.

"Crazy bear. Gone loco. We must leave here immediately. It's evil and will hunt us down to seek revenge. It has followed me even while I was in the deep woods. I knew there was something there. Had a dream about it. Come. Pack!" Esaugetuh said with an urgency I had not heard before. With effort, I finally got to my feet and much to my joy,

Esaugetuh was his normal size. He was looking at me with his piercing azure blue eyes. They bore into me, searching me. Then they softened.

"My god, what did you do? The fire, where did it come from?" I stammered ever mindful of my queasy stomach. "Pack up? Where are we going?"

"Head down river and we'll circle back on foot to your vehicle. We must leave this area completely."

Staggering like a typical drunk, I somehow managed to pick up what was left of our gear. Fortune smiled on us because the skiff was still in one piece. I got the gear loaded in spite of my uncooperative legs and stomach. During this time, Esaugetuh stood, arms folded across his broad chest, staring off into the night at the woods. I wondered what thoughts were going through his mind.

Shit! I can't believe how stupid I am. I just witnessed the power of a shaman and didn't even recognize it. What a jerk! Instead of asking what it was he did, which was obvious, I should have asked how he did it and would he teach me how to do that. No wonder he says I don't know how to ask the question.

"You're right on both counts. That skiff ready? If it is, let's get going."

"And you read people's minds, too?"

"Just get in and get into the center of the river. Be quick about it."

We floated down river ending up at Concrete; a sleepy little down nestled along the Skagit River. A movie with Leonardo DiCaprio featured Concrete, so named because of its main industry, the manufacture of concrete. Esaugetuh had decided that it was not a good idea to hike back up toward Marblemount and our car. I was able to hire a guy to drive us there. After stashing what was left of our gear into the Cherokee, I turned it around and headed west to pick up the interstate. At Burlington, we picked up I-5 and I headed north toward Vancouver, British Columbia. Other than telling me to head north, Esaugetuh had been very quiet. I thought he was actually sleeping but that turned out not to be the case.

"Turn around. Head back south. There's a state park on a small island just south of Mount Vernon. Go there. Better stop and refurbish the supplies. To answer your earlier question, yes, I can read your mind. I should say your thoughts. I will teach you how to prevent that so you will be comfortable around me. Oh, don't worry, I'm not a snoop. It's just that sometimes your thoughts are so strong they simply leave themselves open."

I found an exit, and then turned around and got back on I-5. We stopped in Mount Vernon picked up some food supplies, a new pop-up tent, and new sleeping bags. I also bought a 30-30 rifle, a couple boxes of flat points and a sixteen gage shotgun and shells. I wasn't about to be out in the woods again without ample firepower. I bought a tin of stick matches, removed three and put them in my small container hanging around my neck. Esaugetuh grunted his approval of that. He handed me a starter block and two fire sticks.

"You think the old ways are best?" I asked.

"No, they just come in handy sometimes when others fail. View some of them as survival tactics, a backup."

He closed his eyes and folded his arms across his chest. I took that to mean no more talk.

CHAPTER TWENTY THREE
THE QUINTESSENTIAL CONNECTION

. . . if you see yourself as a creator—then you start to share some of God's functions. You stand on more equal ground, until finally, at the stage of "I am," the same pure being is common to both God and humans.
Deepak Chopra
(How to Know God)

Glancing over at Esaugetuh I noticed he seemed tired, weakened, and ashen faced. His eyes were closed and I thought for the first time how very old he really was. His skin had lost it elasticity; wrinkles had set in. Maybe they had been there all along. His mouth seemed drawn, dry and lifeless; cracks appeared at its corners. Even his white hair, once neat and shiny, seemed tangled and dull. As we zipped along in the jeep I wondered who this stranger was sitting beside me.

I hit the exit to Stanwood/Camano Island State Park a little too fast and had to slam on the brakes. The jolt brought Esaugetuh to rapt attention, yet he said nothing. According to the sign, Camano Island was eight miles out of Stanwood. The main road actually by-passed the town so I didn't get to see much. The names of a few stores I could see from the road suggested it was a Scandinavian town in its origins.

As I crossed the bridge to the island it struck me that it was the only way on or off the fifteen mile long island. Hell of a note if there was an emergency. The state park was at the end of the island and its entrance was marked by an all too small sign. I nearly missed it. A narrow paved road brought us into the park. On my left was the park ranger's house. Esaugetuh had me stop. He went in and had arranged for us to pitch camp as close to the water as permissible.

As Esaugetuh got back into the Cherokee I asked, "Any bears on this island?"

"Not to my knowledge. Coyote, raccoon, deer and maybe a cougar or two. To ease your concern, can't we use the jeep as our bed? No need to set up the tent."

I thought about that. Esaugetuh had never used the tent and neither had I. Not sure why I bought another one. I pulled into a spot he indicated, stopped, set the brake, and proceeded to unload the jeep. I folded down the back row of seats, placed the sleeping bags, and then set up two folding chairs. No more sitting on the ground.

The sun well into its setting path broadcast a pallet of artist's colors reflected on calming waters. Snowcapped mountains, White Horse and Three Fingers, glistened in the evening sun and seem to have been spray-painted on the horizon, a backdrop for a Western movie. Just to my left, I could see Mount Baker, looking very much like a large dish of vanilla ice cream with one spoonful taken out. There was something special about it even though it was not nearly as high as Mount Rainer. Like a magnet, it held my gaze. And just for a moment, I felt my soul fly out to it, greet its beauty and return. I heard myself gasp.

This would be a tranquil time for most people. It was anything but peaceful for me. I felt like there had been a massive explosion within my being, sending me off into a vast unknown universe where I was being sucked into a giant black hole. I couldn't shake the dream I had of being covered with mud and leaves and roasted over a fire. I looked at my right hand. There was still tenderness in its palm as I rubbed a finger over the small spot that had been covered with mud. I sensed answers to my expanding questions were close; the anticipation of finally knowing and the potentiality of it all were agonizing. Yet, there was a heightened delight, a wonderful sense of excitement. I was so engrossed in my own world I didn't realize I was pacing up and down the stony beach until I felt Esaugetuh's hand on my shoulder. I stopped and looked directly at his eyes and as I did I was reminded of the poem, *Footprints upon the Sand* and wondered how much longer he would carry me.

"Sit," Esaugetuh said as he motioned his hoary head toward the two chairs I had set up. "Remember our discussion about the stars?"

"Sure. You said the dust of those stars is a part of every one of us and has been since the beginning of our existence. And that the light we see is past-time light, yet it is here, now, real for all who take the time to look at it."

"Good. There are things even beyond that existence. Things that are just now beginning to be revealed, to be known and understood," Esaugetuh said.

"For instance?"

"Before I get into that, I had said I would come back to the issue of the self, of the *I* of *I-Am*. The value of self has been damned, laid out, slaughtered upon the altar of the righteous, and declared as that which *ought to be denied* by certain Christian groups. It has been an object of self-destruction, of self-mutilation, and self-immolation by certain Buddhist groups, and finally it has been laid upon the couch of psychoanalysis. Earlier, I said Prometheus foreshadowed Buddha-thinking and that is true, but only to a point. He stops at guided flow. At no time does he indicate the destruction of the self, the *I of I-Am*.

Some Buddhist, for example, hold a belief indicating that all suffering comes from the notion that there are inherently and independently existing objects and subjects, and that any identifiable level of subjectivity is empty of independent existence. Now, to alleviate this, the 'doctrine of emptiness' has been advanced. This is the denial of the *I* of *I-Am*. Yet, to do so, they must exist and that existence consists of an I, as self, as an Ego.

As far as I am concerned, this is tantamount to denying your existence. Part of my task, as far as you are concerned, is to bring about a denial of your nothingness. Certainly not to make you an Indian."

"Denial of my nothingness? What the hell do you mean by that? And if you have adopted me, doesn't that make me an Indian?"

"By denial of your nothingness I mean you have been conditioned to deny the value of self, of ego. Your white culture has done that. Your religions have told you that it is not good to think of the self. Your educators have taught you that it is better to sacrifice self for the good of the many. In sports, you are taught the individual must exist for the benefit of the team. And that same abomination has carried over into the professional and business worlds. Unfortunately, you have come to believe it is necessary to kill the *I* of *I-Am*, that wonderful, fulfilling selfsame self so absolutely essential for survival. Without this self, this marvelous *I* of the *I-Am*, there would have been no Buddha to search the world for a cure for mankind's suffering, no Ovid or Plato, no Shakespeare or Thoreau, no Descartes or Salk. There would have been no discovery of America without this infectious self. There would have no man on the moon or people on a planetary station called Mir. And yes, no Christ to suffer for the masses. The denial of self is the most heinous crime ever set upon mankind, the cruelest joke of all. You must deny this nothingness by loudly proclaiming, I AM!

"What you're saying is that I should be egotistical, self-centered."

"No! By all the spirits of my ancestors, aren't you listening? Without the self, there is no creativity, no invention, no art, no music, and no solution. Like Prometheus, you are a creator god. Only humans are creator gods. Oh, I recognize this sounds like blasphemy. What I'm talking about is not unlike observers of nonlocality in quantum physics. You must first *create the world* by the very act of an observing self, an individual, unique and magnanimous—one who has a shot at this canvas we call life, otherwise there is a true emptiness, a nothingness. I for one am not interested in nothingness," Esaugetuh said.

A woman's cry for help broke our conversation. I looked up and saw her running toward us. I don't' know where she came from. There were no other vehicles or people around.

"Please, please help me! My son. He's hurt."

"Where is he?" Esaugetuh asked, nodding his head in acknowledgement.

"There, along the base of the cliff. He fell from up there," she said, pointing a distance from us. "I can't get him to answer. Please hurry."

"Get into the jeep," I said, as I jumped in and started the engine.

It was getting dark and I knew we had to get him out of the trees and soon. He didn't respond to his mother's calls. I grabbed a rope out of the back of the jeep, slung it over my shoulder and began to climb up the cliff. Several times I slipped as I grabbed one tree or scrub to help pull myself up the steep incline. Finally, I was at the base of the tree in which the boy was lodged. He was caught in a fork of the tree, a large evergreen. I climbed up as far as I could, and then began to use the rope. Tossing it over higher branches I used it to help me climb up to the next level.

When I got to him I called his name, "Sam."

He opened his eyes. Looked at me and began to whimper. I noticed blood at the corner of his lips and that wasn't good. "Internal injuries," I thought.

With effort I had him out of the crook of the tree, taking care not to do any more damage to him.

"Make a sling. Lower him down," Esaugetuh said. "You do know how to make a sling don't you?"

I got a sling up under his arms, and slowly began to lower him down through the branches of the evergreen. Fortunately, it was a soft Hemlock. Esaugetuh had him and laid him on the ground. From my perch in the tree, I watched him pass his hands over the limp body of the little boy. Just for an instant, I thought I saw them glow. The boy wasn't more than five years old. He opened his eyes and seeing Esaugetuh's long white hair he said, "Am I dead, God?"

"No, son. You are not dead. You're bad hurt, but you seem to be pretty tough," Esaugetuh said. Turning to the mother, Esaugetuh continued, "Did you call 911?"

"No reception here. I tried to stop a car up on the road but they wouldn't help me," she was sobbing.

Once I was back on the beach, we loaded the boy and his mother into the jeep and took off up to the park ranger's place. From there a call was made and within a few minutes, a rescue vehicle with paramedics arrived. The bloody mouth was from biting his tongue. They would take him to a hospital at Mount Vernon.

As the mother climbed into the back of the ambulance I asked, "Would you tell me your name. I'd like to call the hospital and see how Sam is doing if it's okay with you?"

"Of course. It's Darlene Oats. And thank you. Thank you!" She said, giving us both a hug.

We went back to the spot where we had been parked. Esaugetuh picked up the conversation right where he had left it.

"There are wonderful holographic potential selves that could come to fruition if they would just stop damning the self. You could be one of those if you would get rid of self-doubt and have faith in yourself. *Faithfulness* is an attribute of Selfhood. Admittedly, it is perhaps the most difficult of the attributes to achieve because of the culture in which you live."

"You sound and act as if you don't live in this culture," I interrupted.

"We are not talking about me! We are talking about you. The culture in which you live breeds self-doubt negates the value of self-worth and preaches a homily of self-sacrifice before an altar called the common good. It's a culture that creates the illusion of freedom and of choice when in reality it wants total conformity."

Interrupting again, I asked, "What do you mean by faithfulness?"

"Faithfulness simply means freedom from self-negation, the freedom from the abyss of nothingness, freedom from the reductionism that prevails throughout much of the world today. It is having no doubts as to your self-worth, the value of your personhood. It is having faith in who and what you are. The alternative to the praise and acceptance of Selfhood is stagnation. Stagnation, which is now the unfortunate situation, will continue to smother the human race until it becomes extinct, not my brothers the spotted owl or the great bald eagle, not my mother the earth, but man! You are stagnant and you're caught up in that acculturated pre-conditioned definition of self, ego, and I. These are not dirty words. It is not a blasphemy to be concerned with the well-being of the self. If it is, then why did your God send his only begotten son to die for you? Did He not value you and see value in you? The joy of living is within the living experience as you create it; mold it, and make it singly your own. Remember, what is created is created out of Necessity. For the self to regain its former station there has to be a change in perspective. Haven't I told you to change your perspective?"

"Only a few hundred times," I said.

"The only connection is the *I-Am*. Look at you. What have you accomplished that has been directed by your own personal self?" Esaugetuh said.

Esaugetuh was getting very personal and I wasn't in any mood for his criticism.

"Not much I dare say. Oh, sure, you went to a fancy Eastern university but wasn't that another's choice? Your career? Isn't this job you have something you just fell into? No real effort on your part. And of course, your relationship with your woman, if you can call it that? Hasn't she made all the initiatives? And what about this trip you're on?" Esaugetuh said, shaking his finger at me.

"At least I'm here. What else matters?" I said, pissed.

I was so pissed at his accusations that I stomped off down the beach. My anger had taken such a hold of me I didn't realize I was wading in waist-deep cold water. The tide had changed. So had I. But was it real or chimerical? I headed back to shore, breaking into a run as I hit shallow water, kicking it with my feet as I ran, feeling its coldness splash against my face.

"Yes!" I screamed, "I am! Yes, I am!"

"Not yet you're not!" boomed a voice from nowhere, yet from everywhere.

CHAPTER TWENTY FOUR
THE FOR INSTANCE

Associate with a wise friend, who detects and censures your faults and who points out virtues as a guide tells of buried treasures.
Dhammapada. Canto VI

Sleep avoided me the way you avoid some guy with bad breath. So I'm a creator? So I have an *I* of an *I-Am*? I am a Self? So I must act out of Necessity, yet force nothing? Flow without control, yet provide direction? Okay. But in hell am I anyway?

"Adam! Adam awakening! That's who."

"What? Who said that? Esaugetuh was that you?" I asked sitting up. "Damn. Nearly knocked myself out. I turned on my flashlight. Esaugetuh was not in the jeep. I crawled out of my sleeping bag. He was outside, sitting cross-legged against the jeep. He was sound asleep.

I wanted to wake him, to ask him but thought better of it. He needed his rest. How he could really sleep like that was beyond me. I pulled a blanket from the back of the Cherokee and wrapped it around him. He never moved. Morning was long coming and as was typical, a mist began to roll in off the water. It filled the air with fresh sea smells and water-sounds as the tide changed. I walked off a bit from the jeep. Stood listening.

An unfathomable emptiness welled up inside of me and chocked me. My chest heaved as I gasped for air. Hyperventilation seized me. An oppressive suffocation strangled my whole being. I tried to call out but could not. Dizziness destroyed my balance and I began to stagger along the rocky beach. A cool breeze swept over me as I floated upon wave after wave of dazzling radiance. Lines from Bob Dylan's song, *The Times They are A-Changin'* traveled my mind like an endless river of metaphoric images.

> *If your time to you*
> *Is worth savin'*
> *Then you better start swimmin'*
> *Or you'll sink like a stone*
> *For the times they are a-changin'.*

I started swimming. God how I swam. Salt water filled my nostrils and sand coated my tongue as I crawled upon the rocks. I felt them tear my skin and I cried out in pain. I struggled to get up. Pain shot through my legs and as I bent to rub them I realized I was naked, stark naked. What the hell had happened to my clothes I have no idea. I stood there, freezing my ass off, looking up at the endless rush of stars and wondered which one contained my soul. For surely it must have been my soul that spoke to me, that *I of me.*

I sat down on a piece of log that had drifted in from some other place, maybe in from a storm, a lost cargo at sea. "Dylan, of course, is right; the times are changing. Like the changing tide in front of me, I too must change. As the ocean cleanses itself, I must cleanse myself of past nonproductive beliefs, of sterile notions, of unfounded biases and valueless hatreds. I must strip bare my falsehoods and stand before all creation, naked as I am, expectant and finally, worthy. But how can I be all that with all the doubts that constantly plague me? Become doubtless. Fine, but how? Ready or not the challenge is here, now, and if I am to survive I must rid myself of the doubt, be mindful and delight in my existence. Above all, I must accept my role as a creator, but creator of what? Now that's a pregnant question."

Out of the heavens themselves came a booming voice, "You have come far, my son. Don't you remember? First, you were mere potter's clay waiting expectantly to be molded into existence. Water and air were added, then fire from the heavens and you became a living entity, and you crawled out of that oceanic womb to ultimately become that which you are— man!

Moreover, during each of these glorious evolutionary stages, you knew neither what you wanted nor where you were going. You just kept wandering, restless in your journey. You have traveled many worlds, splendid and magnificent, but there are still millions of spectacular worlds for you to travel so do not despair, an untold number of experiences await you. Hold fast to what you are! You are to create a new world of conscious evolution—one which all human beings can free themselves from their conditioned assertions; can free themselves from their false assumptions and can free themselves from their nothingness. Return mankind to the sacredness of the *I-Am* so that it may know the wonder of its own being. All this, my son, you must do not in my name, but your own! Then you will know that which you seek!"

"Esaugetuh! Where are you? Is that you talking? Damn it, answer me!" I screamed.

Just above my head, there was a swoosh sound. Instinctively I ducked. Then a loud thud. Just a few feet away flopping around on the beach were two adult eagles engaged in a fight to the death. Even though their talons were locked together they continued to strike at each other with their beaks, beating at each other with their huge wings. They would stay that way until they died. I wondered what had caused such anger, such violence in such beauty. What was it that had transpired that both were willing to die for whatever perceived injustice? Man certainly isn't any different.

Then out of the sea fog strode a figure. Esaugetuh. Ignoring me, he went to the eagles, passed his hands over them. Their flapping wings stilled; they calmed themselves. He bent down, picked them up, and lifted them above his head and with a shake; he tossed them into the air. Freed of each other, each flew off in different directions. A loud shrill call penetrated the quiet and Esaugetuh with his arms stretched skyward, answered them. Once again a flutter of powerful wings came awfully close to my head and I heard a second thud on the ground.

"Breakfast," Esaugetuh said, picking up the salmon dropped by the eagle. "And put some clothes on. This isn't a nudist colony. We're at a public park. Clean yourself up. You look a mess. Why are you covered in blood?"

I walked back into the water, swam for a time, came back out and much to my surprise there wasn't one scrape to be found on my body. The stones and shells along the beach made walking barefoot a challenge. By the time I got back to the jeep, I no longer noticed any discomfort they caused. Esaugetuh had the salmon cleaned and cooking by the time I got my clothes on. My cell phone was on the seat and it reminded me that I had said I'd call to see how the boy was.

After getting the number from Information I called the Mount Vernon hospital. Much to my surprise, Sam answered the telephone. He was a regular little chatter box, telling me in detail how he had slipped and was caught by the tree. Darlene was exuberant. There were no broken bones and what was really amazing was the lack of any bruising. She wanted to know about Esaugetuh because she recalled he had passed his hands over her son.

"He's a healer," I said.

"And you?" Darlene asked.

"I'm his adopted son," I replied as we said good bye. I wondered when I had stopped thinking of my own parents.

The smell of the baking salmon coaxed me back to the fire pit. I devoured the plate of food Esaugetuh handed me. As I licked my lips from the last bite, Esaugetuh picked up the remaining fish and went to the edge of the water. He knelt down, placing the leftover fish into the water he spoke in a strange language. When he stood up and turned to come back to the fire pit, I thought I caught a glimpse of a tear at the corner of his eye. I didn't ask but somewhere in the far reaches of my brain I remembered some Indians returned the remains of the animals they killed for food to their natural habitat. They did that out of respect and gratitude. I simply had not noticed Esaugetuh doing that before but I'm sure he had done so with everything we had eaten. 'Respect all existence,' he had said, 'even that which nourishes you.'

I wanted to ask Esaugetuh about my latest episode as well as the *dream* of being held over burning coals. I didn't get the chance.

"Pack up. We go to sacred grounds," Esaugetuh said. "When you're finished, get back on I-5 and head south. I'll tell you when and where to stop."

Just like that. No explanation. His erratic behavior was concerning me: the long periods of silence, the change in locations, the barked orders. The whole business with the bear and with the little boy, Sam. Add to that his apparent ability to read my mind. He has yet to show me how to block that. Each time I get a sense of well-being, a sense of understanding he pulls the rug out from under me, so to speak. Dutifully I packed up the Cherokee and as directed, we headed north off the island and on to Interstate 5.

First Everett, then Seattle, next Tacoma, and then Olympia became nothing more than mere blurs along the evergreen landscape. Silence was my companion. Esaugetuh stared straight ahead, his hands folded on his lap, and no expression on his face. Out of boredom, I slipped a CD into the player. I didn't pay any attention to the selection but it brought Esaugetuh out of his stance. A hauntingly beautiful instrumental, *Apology to the Animals*, by Stephen Whynott, surrounded us. I looked at Esaugetuh and noticed his expression had softened and a personal peace engulfed him. Whynott's music does that to you. I wondered if I would ever find such serenity.

"Yes, you will know serenity," Esaugetuh said, breaking his silence for the first time in hours. "It's the fifth attribute of Selfhood. It will flow naturally from the center of your inner being and as you openly express the value and worth of the Self, a wellspring of contentment will encompass you, rushing over you and bathing you in a sense of total peace."

"You did it again. Reading my thoughts. Anyway, such a peace would be some feeling. I just don't know if that's possible for me."

"There have always been special places— sacred to both man and animals," Esaugetuh said. "Each place exists for a reason and each has its own special purpose for existing. The Ancient Ones of ages long past told of powerful and mysterious powers existing in these special areas. They told that a man sometimes might find his center in one of these places and come away with peace in his heart and soul. And sometimes there is a transfer of special powers if the quest is noble and pure. We go to such a place, a power center. To be welcome there certain preparations must be made and because of its sacredness, all preparations must be made with the greatest of care. This holy of holy places must be treated with the greatest of respect and dignity. To bring insult to the spirits will be met with severe consequences. Even I do not dare to make challenge."

"What do you have to do to prepare for this *power center* of yours?"

"You. Not me. Your time has come. The signs have so indicated and you have to make a decision and you must carefully prepare—,"

Cutting him off I blurted, "What the hell do you mean, my time has come? Prepare for what, my death? You are freaking me out."

"That depends entirely on you. For some who make the journey, it is death; others find peace, and others, a special few, find rebirth."

I suddenly had a very strong need to urinate. I pulled the Cherokee off to the side of the road, got out, and relieved myself. I leaned back against the jeep. My mind was a tornado, whirling, spinning nonstop. I'd been working on this story for several months. Oh, I know it pales when compared to the amount of time others have spent working a story, yet it feels I've been working on this one all of my life. It has just occurred to me that it's turning out to be my story and not that of Esaugetuh. "As my time draws near, whatever the hell that may or may not mean, I really wonder if I will finally be able to sing '*yes, I am* and actually know the I of me and be fulfilled."

Opening the door, Esaugetuh yelled, "You gonna stand out there all day?"

"We need to gas up," I said, getting back into the jeep.

I pulled into a gas station and man came out and began to pump the gas. While the tank was being filled he cleaned the windshield. He even offered to check under the hood. I went inside, picked up a few snacks, and two coffees. As I was paying the cashier, she said, "Welcome to Oregon."

Shit, I didn't even realize we were in Oregon. Once back in the Cherokee I said,

"Tell me more about this power center you're taking me to. Where is it? What's it like? What kind of power are you talking about?"

"You ever ask just one question? It's a sacred place, home to very important spirits who are the source of great power. These spirits, though governed by natural laws, can take physical form. To even consider approaching them you first must be in a balanced state. That is a state in which you are in harmony with your surroundings and with all creatures, with the great heavens as well as with Mother Earth. The winds of the Four Corners must be aligned in such a way as to play just the right music in your soul. The winds are approaching that phase and you must make up your mind and if you decide to continue you must be ready. The planets must be aligned to allow symmetry of being and they are positioning themselves even as I speak."

"My god! What are you talking about? Balance, harmony, winds, planets, symmetry?"

"Let's being with symmetry. Do you understand symmetry?" Esaugetuh said, unruffled by my frustration.

"Sure, it means proportionally balanced."

"Yes, that's correct, but it means more than just proportion. Symmetry involves a relationship characteristic of correspondence, that is, there is compatibility, an identity among certain constituents or parts. At this time there is a symmetry developing in the heavens. The moon and eight planets [26] will align themselves. To earthbounders, they will appear like a jeweled necklace. It is at that moment of equivalence that the greatest energy is created in the power center, the sacred place where you must be."

"What's going to happen to me?" I asked.

"I really don't know," Esaugetuh said.

"You don't' know! What kind of an answer is that?"

"Nothing could happen to you; on the other hand, you could be in grave danger."

Not liking his choice of the word, 'grave,' I asked, "Do you mean physically?"

"Yes and spiritually. You could have your soul ripped from you."

"Now what kind of shit are you giving me?"

"Change that attitude. And do it now! Anytime you present yourself to the spirits with anger in your heart that anger violates the power center by causing a serious breakdown in the required harmony. That could be most detrimental to you, personally, as it will come back at you seven fold." Esaugetuh said. "It could destroy you."

"Powerful stuff, huh."

"Don't be condescending. It's more powerful than you can imagine. This is not a game. What you are about to undertake is very, very serious business. It is so serious I need your assurance that you will do exactly as I tell you. Violate my instructions, fail to heed them you may end up dead, or worse. You could become a blithering idiot, incapable of coherent speech. You must make a commitment. No pretense."

"I didn't mean to be disrespectful. It's just that I—.

"Just what? Spit it out. Now's the time," Esaugetuh said.

"I'd like more specifics other than words such as power, serious, and dangerous. They tell me nothing of what is to take place," I replied.

"All I can tell you is that you will meet very powerful spirits. I can't tell you how you will react to them or how they will react to you. I do know that they will sense insincerity, pretense, and cowardliness."

"Well, I've come this far. I'll do whatever you say I should do. You've got my word."

"Good. First, we must purify ourselves. This will take four days from now. Not only must our bodies be cleansed but so must our hearts, minds, and souls. We must rid ourselves of all negative influence. I say we because I go to the power center with you. I will be your guide as long as the spirits allow me to do so."

"Okay. When do we begin?"

"We already have."

CHAPTER TWENTY FIVE
PREPARATION

Forget all the worldly knowledge that thou hast acquired . . . then will thou get the divine wisdom.
Ramakrishna

At Esaugetuh's direction, I pulled into an older motel somewhere along the Oregon coast. It was actually a series of seven cabins. For a moment I thought it was deja vu all over again. The cabins were clapboard with small porches and single windowed. The only outward difference from the cabins in Florida was the geographic setting. We were on the Pacific Ocean. A common walkway connected all of the cabins. The beach was an easy stone's throw from our cabin. Immediately after I had signed us in Esaugetuh left, saying he needed to stretch his legs. The unpacking was left up to me. Admittedly, the thought had crossed my mind that I was the mule, packing, unpacking. But then, Esaugetuh did all the cooking.

There was a small wood-burning fireplace in one corner of the cabin. I had noticed a sign at the office saying they had wood for sale. Old fashion twin beds, the kind with white metal headboard, occupied the main wall. A small table, two chairs, one lamp with a wobbly shade with a faded picture of a seascape on its front side made up the rest of the furnishings. There was a shower made of galvanized tin. It, like the rest of the cabin, had seen its better days. The owners, whoever they were, followed the adage if it works, keep it. Since there wasn't a stove or refrigerator I assumed guests were expected to eat at one of the local eateries.

Once I had our gear inside and the jeep secured I went out onto the small porch. I looked out at the Pacific Ocean. Its incoming waves gently lapped at the sandy beach. Time stopped for a while as I listened to the peaceful ocean-song, pulsing the rhythmic pattern, the heartbeat of the earth. I scanned the water hoping to see some ship passing by. Instead of a ship, I saw a huge rock, haystack-shaped— a lonely sentinel fastened against the skyline. It struck me as being prideful of its personal duty as guardian of the sandy shoreline. White foam splashed out from its giant sides and at its top stood a lone figure with outstretched arms. For a moment I thought I was hallucinating or being kicked into another one of my weird experiences. I went back inside, grabbed a pair of binoculars from my stuff and rushed back onto the porch. It was Esaugetuh and in full Indian regalia. I could see the single feather of his headband move in time with the ocean breezes. He made quite the Hollywood figure standing there, expect this wasn't a movie. He began to dance. I was sure I heard him chanting even above the wave sound of the ocean.

The ocean seemed to be moving faster. It suddenly got darker. Thunder rolled across the sky and a brilliant flash filled the sky. I made a dash inside. A ball of sizzling lightening rolled around the room, circling me as it went. I'd always heard that when in the presence of balled lightening you should not move. Even if I had wanted to, I'm not so sure that I could have moved. Seven times it rolled around the room, each time coming closer to where I was standing. Then at the very moment, I was sure it was going to strike me, it shot out the still open cabin door. Ozone burned my nostrils; my eyes filled with tears and I was sure I smelled burnt hair. Mine!

My whole being quivered. Painful tingling shot through my arms and traveled to my fingers. I shook my hands, opened and closed my fingers. My breathing steadied. During this struggle to compose myself, I managed to look about the room and there visible for all to see, were seven perfect circles scorched into the old wooden floor, each coming closer to the spot where I was still standing. The hair on the nape of my neck and arms stood straight up. I bolted from the cabin, jumped down the worn stone steps two at a time until I was on the beach.

Racing along the beach, I strained to see if Esaugetuh was still on the rock. Because the sand was wet from the tide it sucked my shoes from my feet. I couldn't see him even as I got closer to the rock. Panic seized me. I looked out at the water to see if I could spot him floating. No sign of him anywhere. I plunged into the ocean and frantically swam out to the rock. It was a puzzle how he got up there. The rock was slippery, covered with seagull droppings. I found a spot I could climb on. It was then that I noticed a rope dangling down the side of the salt-worn façade.

I grabbed the rope, gave it a yank to make sure it would hold me, and then clambered up monkey style. I slipped a couple of times and swung out over the water. Finally, I reached the top. Esaugetuh was motionless. My heart skipped at least twenty beats. He ignored me as I stood there gasping for breath. After what seemed a life time, he motioned for me to sit and remembering his earlier admonition, I did as I was told. My breathing quieted as did the swirling waters around the rock. The waves now gently caressed the rock, providing its tired exterior a massage. A seagull flew by complaining that it had dropped its meal.

When I had finished my rushed explanation of the lightening ball and the burned seven rings, Esaugetuh stood up. In his hand was a long stemmed pipe. Noting my quizzical expression he broke his silence.

"I offer up a pipe to the spirits of the Four Corners. This is a prayer pipe filled with red willow bark tobacco. Holding the pipe in both hands, he turned to the North. Raising his arms up to the Northern sky Esaugetuh said, "I offer you my pipe our brother in honor of your special place from which we have journeyed out of darkness into the light of our brother, the East."

Next, he turned to the East and holding up the pipe he said, "To you our brother, home of the rising sun in whose direction we travel. We ask for your continued guiding light." Turning to the South and offering up the pipe, Esaugetuh said, "To you our brother from which the warm winds flow. We ask you to continue to smile upon us." And finally turning to the West and holding the pipe high above his head, he said, "To you our brother, home of the setting sun, and the place to which all things flow. We ask that your winds blow gently the wisdom we seek."

Handing me the pipe, Esaugetuh indicated I should smoke it. I inhaled as I slowly drew on the long stemmed pipe. As I inhaled the sweet smelling smoke I felt a new calmness work its way through my body. Maybe it was just my imagination, but whatever, I felt better. I carefully returned the pipe to Esaugetuh, making sure its bowl was pointed away from his heart. That was something I had observed at Mesa Verde. He nodded his head approvingly.

Esaugetuh then carefully laid down seven braids of sweet grass, their heads pointing inwards, forming a perfect circle. He passed his right hand over the grass and it burst into flames. Its sweetness filled the air around us, a welcome relief from the smell of bird poop.

"What about the lightening? Man, it nearly got me."

"That's a good sign. You're still alive, aren't you? Now we begin the purification. Smudge the smoke. Esaugetuh instructed.

"I don't understand," I whispered.

"Use your hands to direct the smoke, first to your head, then to your heart, and then to your abdomen. In the old days, there'd be a feathered fan. Get closer to the fire."

I watched Esaugetuh and copied his rhythmic motions. All sky and water disappeared from my vision. And just as quickly it was all there in front of me once again. Esaugetuh was chanting.

Make us worthy enough to join our Brothers before us;
Worthy enough to join those who will come after,
Make us, as we would be, seated under the Great Council Oak,
Pure of thought, pure of spirit, pure of heart.

Then he handed me a rounded stone, cupped at its center and containing liquid. He indicated that I should drink it. I did.

"What the hell was that? It's awful!" I complained.

"Yellow dock. It'll cleanse your body."

It amazed me that he was able to rappel down the rock with such agility. He had a small leather bag attached to his side. He turned it so it was on his back. Once we were both down, we swam back to shore and headed back to our cabin. There I showed Esaugetuh the burnt circles on the floor and the spot where I was standing when the balled lightening came rolling in. He shook his head and then looked at me with a bemused smile. One little detail he failed to mention was that we would be fasting.

I spent most of the night married to the toilet seat. Morning found Esaugetuh again in prayer. Being respectful of his traditions, I waited for him to speak. I was sure the growling in my empty gut must have penetrated his thoughts because it was so damn loud.

"Drink water. Two glasses," Esaugetuh said without looking up.

I did as I was told. I could hear it slosh around in my stomach.

"You must pray," Esaugetuh said.
"I don't pray."
"You will now."
"But I don't know—,"
"Simply ask the Spirits to guide you and they will. Look for a sign."

It was my turn to beach walk. The sun was breaking and the dimensional clouds reflected its rays coloring the ocean in a glorious radiance. Some distance from our cabin I sat down and just looked out at the vastness of the Pacific, drinking in the morning sea-freshness.

Praying? I thought, what do I know about praying? Okay, I'll pray. That's what Esaugetuh says I have to do. It sure would have helped had he told me what to pray for.

I continued to just sit there. Nothing came. Silences filled my head. Even the morning sounds were denied entrance to any awareness. Numbness crawled over my being. Being? More likely a non-being. Beings feel. I was feeling nothing. Then I heard.

Lines from a Neil Diamond song. Clearly and distinctly they spoke to me.

I am I said and no one was there
And no one heard me at all; not even the chair
I am I cried. I am said I.
And I am lost and I can't even say why. [27]

"All I want to know is the *I of me*. Just give me a sign, some direction or guidance," I said aloud.

And no one was there!

I felt something brush against my face. Thinking it was a bug of some kind I wiped my face. When I got up to head back to our motel cabin I looked down at my feet, a habit I acquired after my episode with the pygmy rattler in Florida. There was an eagle's feather. I looked around, searched the sky. Nothing. I picked it up, slipped it inside my windbreaker.

I wonder? Is this is my sign? If so, what does it mean? Eagles seem to be part of my presence ever since Esaugetuh pointed one out to me on the mountain at Mesa Verde. Maybe I'm to take flight. Get the hell out of Dodge as they say. Damn!

At the cabin, I found Esaugetuh had packed our belongings. And that surprised me.

"This eagle's feather floated down from the sky, touched my face. Is this my sign? If so, what does it mean?" I asked.

"Eagles are a very good sign. They represent many good qualities: wisdom, foresight, strength, and spirituality. Generally if one comes near while you are praying it means that your prayer will be answered. You have experienced eagle gifts several times. I don't know what the gift of the feather means but I do know that it is very important. Guard it and keep it with you at all times. You will know what to do with it when the time comes. Come. It's time to leave. We go to Lake Tahoe."

Fortunately, I had paid only for the night and day with the understanding we were on a day to day basis. We had not gone far along the Oregon coastline when Esaugetuh ordered me to stop the Cherokee. I pulled to the side of the road.

"Get out and look up at the sky," Esaugetuh said.

I got out and looked up at the sky. Thousands of wild geese heading north. The usual V-shape flight pattern was missing. The whole image was different. Not what I had expected. It was a collage of hexagons and octagons inner connected with long strings of geese intersecting into and out of the traditional flight pattern.

Tuning to Esaugetuh who had the window rolled down I said, "Looks like they got into corn liquor rather than just corn."

"Don't be irreverent. This is another mysterious sign. Like the double ring of ice crystals around the sun, the birth of the white buffalo, the loco bear, the balled lightening, and the gift of the eagle's feather. And now this. Very strange."

As I climbed back into the jeep I asked, "Where are we staying at Tahoe?"

"We're not. We go into the deep woods.

"I guess we better stop and get some additional supplies. How long are we going to be camped out there?"

"No need for them. Just bottled water. Speaking of water, you need to have a drink of this tea. It contains necessary nutrients," Esaugetuh said, handing me a cup.

I swallowed it in one gulp expecting something bitter. To my surprise, it had a pleasant taste. I didn't bother to ask what was in it.

"I'll keep your stomach quiet. Tell me how do you feel?"

I wanted to say with my hands but knew better. "I'm okay."

"I mean for you to be specific. Any dizziness, blurring of your vision, headache, blood in the urine?"

"No. I'm fine. Hungry, but I notice even that seems to be dissipating. The tea helped. Thanks."

Esaugetuh who had slept much of the way decided that he would take over and drive the rest of the way into Lake Tahoe. It would be dark by then. I was actually grateful for the opportunity to get out and stretch my long legs. Once back in the jeep I was soon asleep. When I woke up morning light was creeping along the horizon. Esaugetuh was not in the jeep. I spotted him sitting on the ground by a picnic table.

"You sleep well?" Esaugetuh asked.

"Yes. How long have you been out here?"

"Not long. You ready to go on?" Esaugetuh asked.

"Sure. Anytime you are."

"You drive," Esaugetuh said.

CHAPTER TWENTY SIX
A QUESTION

*As questions from your heart and you will be
answered from the heart.*
Omaha saying

I didn't get in the jeep. I stood there looking out at the Lake. We were parked at one of the many roadside picnic areas. Esaugetuh was respectful of my silence thinking that I was praying. I was not. I had a burning question I wanted him to answer. I wanted his answer before we continued.

Finally, I blurted, "Esaugetuh is there a god? You talk about spirits and mystical powers. Do you believe there is a GOD?"

"Wondered when you were going to ask that. Actually, you've asked me two questions. The saying 'To thine own self be true' is appropriate because by Necessity I first of all have to be honest with myself. As a fellow traveler in this cosmology, my immediate answer is a resounding no!"

"I'll be damned. I was sure you believed in God despite all your spirit talk."

"Don't just to conclusions. Again you have not asked the right question," Esaugetuh said, shaking his head. I said no and I believe, I know that humans are spiritual beings. What I am saying no to is the blond-haired blue-eyed Jesus, the kindly white haired old man sitting on a golden throne that has been crammed down civilization's throat for over 2000 years. I say no to the concept of a Mohammed sitting with 70 virgins in a golden palace, of a Brahma lying upon a silken couch with a sprouting Lilly emerging from his navel or any other singular anthropomorphic rendition of deity."

"So you're saying you don't believe in a supreme being?" I asked.

"No, I am not. I am not saying I do not believe in an infinite creator, that infinite mystery, that wonder of wonders. Of course, I recognize that mankind has struggled for many millennia to give definition to that which is the ground of our being; that it has given over to metaphor the responsibility of description," Esaugetuh said.

"Metaphor? Description?"

"The problem, at least it seems that way to me, arises when we believe in the metaphor and not that for which it stands. And isn't that the fundamental issue in today's theologies? They have forgotten what the metaphor stands for."

"Do you believe that man has a soul, that I have a soul? You said these spirits that I may encounter could rip out my soul. Man, that's heavy," I said.

"Adam, I believe that man has a soul. Absolutely. I also believe that it is integrated into the human being upon its conception. It seems to me that the soul naturally seeks its place of conception—that infinite mystery—that wonder of wonders."

"What do you mean 'seeks its place of conception'?"

"When the soul leaves the body, death as you call it, it is born that is, expelled from the body just as the child is expelled from its mother's womb. The metaphor got twisted when we called such a process death. The soul returns to the infinite."

"Why?" I asked.

"Why what?" Esaugetuh replied.

"Why does the soul seek its infinite origin?"

"It does so because it is an inherent part of human nature."

"Okay, so what is this inherent nature?" I asked, totally mesmerized by Esaugetuh's answers. Finally, I thought, some answers.

"Man's inherent nature is his spirituality."

This time I was the one with tears. I tried blinking them away so Esaugetuh wouldn't notice. This was the first time I had ever had a sense of what it meant to be complete. I felt secure. And it felt good.

"We better move on," Esaugetuh said. "Head northeast."

CHAPTER TWENTY SEVEN
DEEP WOODS

When you feel the universe flowing directly through you, you will cease to feel longing or lacking.
John David Brich
(Flux and Flow)

Some distance outside of the city of Lake Tahoe, Esaugetuh told me to pull off the road. We were in an area directly above the lake. Esaugetuh remained silent during our hike into the deep woods. Finally, we entered a natural clearing surrounded by a circle of large evergreens, some of which were more than a hundred feet tall. They were stately guardians forming a natural cathedral, a sanctuary from the rest of the world—a sanctuary whose stillness was only broken by an occasional birdcall. The smell was intoxicating, clean, refreshing. For a precious moment, I was sure these elegantly dignified giants were making words about us, tossing them into the air, whisperings of things yet to come.

Esaugetuh walked to the center of the clearing and looked around.

"Now we begin. First, we must find seven sacred stones. Each must be circular and each no more than seven inches in diameter," Esaugetuh announced.

"How do I know one stone from another? A stone is a stone for Christ's sake?"

"You'll know. Sacred stones are warm to the touch. And stop being disrespectful. You are on sacred ground."

"Disrespectful? I'm not being dis—,"

"Stop the cussing, the swearing, cursing. And it is to stop now! You understand?"

"Okay. Gees you have to get bent all out of shape."

"Hunt for the stones. Time is important."

I began scurrying around on my hands and knees looking for stones and not really knowing what it was I was looking for. Those that I picked up and met Esaugetuh's criteria of seven inches in diameter didn't feel warm. I was fast tiring of this little treasure hunt. I picked up a likely looking candidate and was about to throw it back when I realized it was actually radiating heat.

"Hey! I think I found one. It's warm. Here feel for yourself," I said.

"I believe you. I've no need to test it for warmth. If you say it feels warm, then it is."

Man, what a grouch, I thought as I continued to scour the ground for warm stones.

Three hours later we had seven warm circular flat stones, each seven inches in diameter. After carefully examining each one, Esaugetuh painstakingly placed each stone in a circle with seven inches separating them. On each stone, he made a strange symbol, Egyptian looking. On the other hand, maybe it was Greek.

Next, he took seven stalks of sweet grass and made them into a teepee and placed that in the center of the circle of stones. Taking something from his medicine pouch, Esaugetuh drew a circle around the sweet grass teepee so that there was now a circle within a circle. He did this six more times. Seven circles with the circle of seven, seven-inch stones laid out seven inches apart. He walked around his creation, checking and double checking his work. Satisfied he sat down in the traditional Indian cross-legged manner. All this time he neither spoke to me or looked at me. It was if I wasn't there.

From his seated position, he called for me to come and sit down. I sat down across from him and imitating his seating position, I sat cross-legged.

"I'll tell you two stories from the history of my people before we begin."

I wasn't really in any mood for story time. My empty gut was growling and I was thirsty. I felt it was better to humor Esaugetuh than to start complaining so I kept my mouth shut. He surprised me by offering me a cup of tea. This time I took my time in drinking it, letting it roll around in my dry mouth before swallowing.

"My brothers, the Chippewa's, have handed down a story of how maze come into existence. It's a very good story but it holds other meanings besides telling how corn came to be. It is the underlying implied message that I want you to understand. It will serve you well as you begin your vision quest."

"Okay. Fire away."

"Many moons ago, more moons than can be remembered, there was a young Indian boy who lived with his parents, brothers, and sisters. His father, a kind man, was a hunter but not always successful at providing for his family. This worried the young boy and he wished with all his young heart that he could do something to help his family, to help his people. Being of the age to seek his guiding spirit, the young boy went to a sweat lodge at some distance from the encampment to begin his fast. He began by offering up prayers in which he asked for ways to help his family and his people. After the traditional days of fasting, he grew weak and fainted. Someone calling his name awakened him.

A handsome youth was challenging the young boy to a fight. He promised the boy that if he won he would grant him his wish. For three long days, they fought. The Indian boy was weak from fasting and was hardly a match for the handsome youth; somehow he managed to stay with the struggle. On the third day, the handsome youth said he had had enough and would grant the young boy his wish.

Of course, as the story goes, the boy said he wanted to feed his family and people during the winter months. The handsome youth instructed the boy to dig up the earth, place him in that dug up earth, to come back and turn the soil over, keep the place watered and weed free. With the arrival of fall the maize had grown. The boy was able to feed his family and his people during the winter months."

"What has that to do with me?" I asked.

"First, the story tells you that your quest must be noble in its nature. Second, you will have to fight your shadow-self. It will be a fierce battle and how you fight your battle depends on how you perceive yourself. If you win you will be granted your wish. If you lose, it may mean your life. If you win, you will have a personal spirit-guide for a lifetime. If you lose and you don't die, you may end up a soulless wanderer. This is a very serious time now. Try to remember some of the things I've told you. You will need to reach to the very abysm of your soul for strength to fight as did the young Indian boy. The will to live is your greatest asset as long as that *will* goes beyond mere raw desire. Are you sure you really want to continue? Think about it carefully, Adam, once you start there is no turning back."

"Let's do it."

"Good. While I tell you my second story, rub this sage over your body and then offer up these tobacco bundles to the spirits," Esaugetuh said, watching me, searching me with those ever penetrating blue eyes of his.

I rubbed the sage over my body as Esaugetuh had instructed.

"Clear your mind of any negative thought while you offer the tobacco. Light each bundle separately, one at a time. Light the second bundle just as the first burns itself out and follow that pattern until all have been offered. Are you ready?"

"Okay. I've done the sage," I replied.

"Good. My second story involves a young Indian who wanted to be a powerful medicine man.

He went on his vision quest to ask the spirits to grant him his wish. What I'm telling you, is a telescoped version. Anyway, this young Indian, without benefit of food or water, spent three days and three nights in a pit. There, he prayed and wailed through the long nights. Sometimes he was filled with total terror as he heard the spirit voices tell him to go away, to stop disturbing them. They told him he was unworthy. Twice he saw a huge boulder come crashing down the mountain toward him. Yet he remained! The third time the boulder came down the mountain the young Indian bolted and ran back to his village. The huge rolling boulder overtook him and he was sure he was about to die. The boulder bounded over him, smashing into the earth with such force that the ground shook for several minutes. When he entered his village and found the elders he informed them that he had learned nothing.

One among the elders made this reply: 'You went after your vision like a hunter after buffalo, or a warrior after scalps. You were fighting the spirits. You thought they owed you a vision. Suffering alone brings no vision nor does courage, nor does sheer will power. A vision comes as a gift born of humility, of wisdom, and of patience.'" [28]

"Are you telling me that the spirits will attempt to destroy me because I am going on a vision quest?" I asked, lighting the last of the tobacco bundles.

"That is not what I am telling you. Think about what I have told you. Listen to the wisdom. Both stories carry good advice and you will need such advice if you are to survive. Do not take lightly what you have started. Once again, remember this is serious business."

Esaugetuh stood up and waved his hand slowly over the sweet grass teepee and then began to chant in low rhythmic voice.

Oh, Great Spirit whose breath makes the Four Winds,
Creator of rain and rainbows, of sunrises and sunsets,
Moon glow and stardust,
Grant this undeserving man the wisdom to know;
To understand and to accept all that you have touched,
To love that which you have given so freely.

Oh, Great Spirit,
Intercessor for all things living and nonliving,
Show this weakling the way to compassion and empathy'
Show him the way to love all that is!
Show him the way to everlasting tranquility.
Grant him the knowledge to survive with dignity and grace.

Oh, Great Spirit
Unworthy as he is, give him a sign of hope.
Make his heart strong as the great winds,

Make him as wise as my brother the owl,
Grant him the courage of the she-bear defending her cubs,
Grant this so he may be whole.

Suddenly the outer circle that surrounded the sweet grass tepee burst into flames. Each of the remaining six inner rings burned one after the other and when they had burned themselves out, the teepee ignited sending up a cylinder of white smoke. I followed its upward path using its cylindrical shape as a telescope. I was fascinated as white nacreous, opalescent orbs became web-like and funneled their way through the treetops, eventually spilling outward until the whole area was wrapped in moon-glow.

Continuing to look skyward I finally saw her, Artemis, goddess of all wild things. I was sure she winked at me. Nearby a low cough, the night voice of a cougar reminded me where I was—in deep woods. Yet even that reminder was not enough to keep my eyelids from growing heavier and heavier until I no longer could keep my them open. As I drifted off, Esaugetuh became a blur and then ceased to exist. All time ceased to exist.

My stomach had long since stopped it growling. Now it just ached, making me believe it was actually eating itself. Thirst bit at my throat as the taste of warm blood bathed my dry tongue. And that brought me wide awake. I had been chewing my own mouth. It seemed to me that there were very quiet moments populated by the murmuring of my own heartbeat. My skin felt clammy and yet I was not cold. I looked at my wristwatch and realized that I had lost seven days. A whole week gone just like that. And nothing. I was ready to screw this whole charade. No boulders had chased me; no one had come to fight me. My head was swirling and it was difficult for me to focus. I tried to see Esaugetuh. He wasn't there. I turned to see if he was sitting somewhere else. And that's when a living hell broke loose.

I was jolted by spasms so severe that I cried out in pain. Jerked violently back and forth I was slammed into the ground so hard that I was sure that every bone in my body had been broken. I screamed. And there was no one there. Yet I was being dragged, dragged downward, slowly at first, and then with such a rush, my life's breath was sucked from me. Dirt flew past me, crumbling as I was dragged deeper into the bowels of the earth. I was sure I was being buried alive.

"No! I'm not dead. I live. I am alive!" I screamed.

That did absolutely no good. The earth's dankness engulfed me and caliginous shadows darted by while others lingered, grotesque things, indefinable, yet snake-like. Each took delight, showing a toothless grin, as each took a swipe at me. The smell they stirred up was worse than the sewers of Paris or London. I chocked, gasped for air as miasmic vapors surrounded me.

Shit! What was it Esaugetuh had said? Remember! Damn it! Remember, I muttered.

From somewhere, way off in the distance, I heard his voice, "Don't under estimate the threat of your shadow-self. Don't hold on to it when it has you in its clutches. Don't fight it. Let go. Remember Prometheus."

"Yes," I thought, "let go." And out of the inner depths of my memory came a recollection of what one should do if caught in an avalanche. I was in an avalanche of tons of dirt. I frantically got myself turned around and began to butterfly. Rocks smashed against my arms, tearing at my flesh. The tormenting shadows blurred as my speed quickened and I was forcibly turned upward and expelled into the open air.

Gulping in its freshness, my lungs ever so grateful for the oxygen, I tried to look around. It was nearly impossible because of the breakneck speed at which I was traveling. I was in the air. I tried to yell; no sound escaped from my gaping mouth. I felt my lips spread across my stretched face. Was I in a centrifuge? I finally managed to look down. I whizzed by South America and Africa was just a blur. For some reason, I hovered over the grand mountains of Tibet and just for a second, I thought I could hear the prayer bells of the monks.

An updraft caught me and I shot past the moon. Many faces were floating in space, their bodies obscured by Cimmerian void. Some were benign faces while others seemed hostile. Gradually the faces became eyes, wide open, lifeless and empty. No feelings could I sense in any of them. And these too changed as I fixed on individual pairs. I saw and felt great sadness and tears welled up inside of my being of being. My chest heaved as I tried to call out them. That was a wasted effort because there wasn't even a faint echo of my voice. It was choked off by obtuse silence.

Galvanizing! Eyes melted into new and different shapes, wolf-like animals and giant birds— eagles speeding by. I was sure I felt the caress of their wing tips against my face. And to keep up with them, my speed increased and I shot past them into a giant maelstrom, sucked in at tremendous speed. All became a dark blur.

With a sudden jerk, I stopped before the most magnificent sight imaginable. Hanging in space I looked out at and down into a fabulous Komodo Dragon's eye consisting of an array of blues. Prussian blue near the outer edge and as I continued my gaze, looking deep into its interior, there were varying shades of blue from lazuli to cerulean. Fire-gold rimmed the eye's edge illuminating its interior. At its center were two bright shiny objects very much like the star-sparkle put in photographs of Christmas lights. There seemed to be no end to its depth. Out of that marvelous celestial eye came naked Sylvan bodies encased in translucent orbs that swirled all around me, embryonic yet something more—Homunculi. [29]

Were they lost souls or souls waiting to be born? They were all faceless until one turned directly to me and there, for the first time, I saw myself, the *I* of me, serene and radiantly at peace. I suddenly realized they were my lives yet to be lived, an endless sperm bank and just for a micron, I thought my shadow-self winked back at me, acknowledging my right to tranquility. I couldn't have been more mistaken!

I was hurled through space again, a vortex out of control. I flew past those eight aligned planets Esaugetuh had told me about and thrown into deep space. Billions of stars as well as whirling, swirling shiny things surrounded me. Some black, some blue-black while others were deep purple. There was an explosion of red-yellow and blue-green in every direction I looked. What a fabulous Fourth of July show bursting across infinite space. A total intoxication! And I had a front row seat. I was so engrossed in the splendiferous panorama unfolding in front of me that I almost didn't hear it.

A melodic baritone was filling all space, all empty space—dimensional and one-dimensional, bent and unbent, collapsed and exploding space simultaneously. I felt its vibrations surround my heart, massaging it into a new rhythmic pattern, synchronized with the heartbeat of the universe itself.

"*Tat tvam ausi at*. You are that!"

"I am what?" I heard myself say, my voice quivering.

"You are the Self of the Universe, the conscious and the unconscious, the *Aham*. [30]

Therefore you are no longer *Sati.*"[31]

"And so I am," I replied.

"And you are all that I am, and I am all that you are, one and the same as Me, Myself and I are!"

I opened my eyes. Esaugetuh was gone and bittersweet loneliness engulfed me. Tears formed and I cried. I don't know how long I cried and I don't know why I cried. It was just something that I did. As I went to wipe my face I realized I still held the eagle's feather in my hand, intact. A flush came over me as I gazed at it and it was then that I realized why I cried. No man can forget where his true interest must be. I had forgotten that. I cried for my Self. The secret of all secrets is to have a passion for who you really are, to have a wondrous and marvelous joy in your aliveness.

The Self is totally and completely inseparable from everything else in all existence and if that is not understood, there is no true viable, validated existence possible.

I realized— I mean really realized— for the first time, that once you have an understanding of who you are, the whole universe unfolds itself and answers to questions are revealed. The Self is a wondrous extension of the universe and therein lays the power to change the world around you. There's the key to true power, realizing that whatever you experience is not the sum of our own perceptions, of your own creations— but a phantasmagoric journey into total reality, explosive and atomic because those experiences are reflective of the universe, of all knowledge, of total being.

Voices interrupted my thought patterns.

"The call that there was a naked guy surrounded by a pale blue light was sitting in a clearing talking to himself. That clearing should be through this thicket. Been a spell since I was in the deep woods this far," the Ranger said.

"You mean what the locals call the Cathedral? The Deputy asked.

"Yeah. Here's the entrance. Sure wonder what this guy is doing out here," the Ranger said.

"Who knows? All kinds of weirdoes are out and about nowadays," said the Deputy.

"There. Jesus. He is glowing. And he's naked as a plucked chicken," the Ranger said.

"My god. You can almost see right through him. You sure he's for real?" said the Deputy.

Once they got closer to Adam they could see he had had a fire. "Must have burned his clothes to stay warm. Gets cold out here at night," the Ranger said.

I said nothing to them. What could I say? As they helped me to my feet and wrapped me in a blanket, I dropped the eagle feather into the circle of seven stones. It fell on the spot where I had been sitting and instantly burst into flames. High above the trees, I heard an eagle's call. Knowing it, I answered with my soul.

One of the last things I remember Esaugetuh saying to me was that 'man exists to receive the highest wisdom from reality and to return that gift through a life of respect and compassion for all sentient beings.'

And so I began my transformation.

FOOTNOTES

[1] Kinnikinnick is a trailing evergreen plant with pinkish-white flowers. Its bright red berries are edible. The dried leaves were smoked by a number of Native American people.

[2] In Greek Mythology, Tantalus was punished by the gods for various crimes, including the killing of his own son and feeding him to the gods. As punishment he was to be eternally tantalized by having his food and water always just out of reach.

[3] A new personification of a familiar idea.

[4] Psychiatrist Stanley R. Dean quoted page 46 in *Mysticism and the New Physics* by Michael Talbot. New York: Bantam, 1981.

[5] Means *Master of Breath*. He is viewed as the life-giving god who created human beings. Muskogean (Creek) tradition. Like Prometheus in Greek Mythology, Esaugetuh Emissee shaped the first humans from the clay of Nunne Chaha, the first hill which rose up from the primeval waters. In Mik'Maq he is Glooscap.

[6] Sanskrit. Means "May you experience the blessing of spiritual love."

[7] A paraphrase from *Zen Flesh, Zen Bone* by Paul Reps. Boston: Tuttle Publishing. 1998.

[8] Hume, Robert, Ernest. (Trans.) From the *Brhad-Aranyanka Upanishad*. 1.3:28. London: Oxford University Press, 1958.

[9] An ancient sacred Hindu text.

[10] Keats, John, *Ode to a Nightingale* in *Word, Meaning, Poem*. Morse Peckham and Seymour Chatman. New York: Thomas Y. Crowell Company, 1961, p. 357

[11] The film, starring the actress, is based on her book, *Out on a Limb*. New York: Bantam, 1983.

[12] In Ancient Egypt the ***ab*** was viewed as the seat of knowledge, that is, what one may know of the world and of himself. Ab is one of the nine Egyptian souls.

[13] Celaladin Mehmet Rumi also known as Jalal ad-Din Muhammad Balkh. A Persian Sufi poet of the 13th Century. Rumi itself is an Arabic word meaning Christian.

[14] From "The Living Come from the Dead" in *Parabola, Winter, 1998, p. 58*

[15] Nicolas Gisin in 1997 demonstrated such a concept. Before Gisin was Alain Aspect in the 1980's.

[16] Sufism asserts God's fundamental unity. Hinduism emphasizes the essential identity of the individual soul with the unqualifiedly Absolute. Sufism and Hinduism are just two such examples.

[17] The Hero with A Thousand Faces. Princeton. Princeton University Press, 1972.

[18] Paul Roche (Trans.). Aeschylus Prometheus Bound. Wauconda: Bolchazy-Carducci Publishers. 1960, p. 36

[19] Depending on the nature of the offense, the offender may be seated, bent over, or upright. Further, it was customary to execute the offender at the frontier of the country, showing rejection by the world to which he had formerly belonged.

[20] Aeschylus.

[21] Aeschylus op.cit.

[22] Arrow-wood is actually Ocean Spray, a very hard wood that grows plentifully in the Northwest United States.

[23] Means a white rump or elk in Shawnee.

[24] Don Juan is the teacher of Carlos Castaneda in *The Teachings of Don Juan: A Yanqui Way of Knowledge*. Berkley: University of California Press, 1968.

[25] Called *camas* and is a member of the lily family. Tastes somewhat like a pear. Since there is a poisonous variety the author does not recommend that you venture into the wilds to locate camas for your own eating. Mistakes are easily made and have deadly consequences.

[26] The eight planets that aligned themselves were Pluto, Mercury, Mars, Venus, Neptune, Uranus, Jupiter, and Saturn. A crescent moon was alongside. The aligned themselves with Earth.

[27] Neil Diamond. *I am I said*. Prophet Music, Inc. ASCAP. 1971.

[28] Richard Erdoes and Alfonso Ortiz. *American Indian Myths and Legends*. New York: Pantheon. 1984. P.72. Originally told by Lame Deer at Winner, Rosebud Indian Reservation, SD, 1967 and recorded by Richard Erdoes.

[29] Homunculi were believed to be miniature adults in the theory of pre-formation and are said to inhabit the sperm cells and will eventually produce mature individuals merely by an increase in size.

[30] Sanskrit meaning 'center'.

[31] Sanskrit meaning 'becoming' as it is used here.

About the Author

Norman W. Wilson was introduced to the world of shamanic healing at the age of seven. He and his teacher, a Mik'Maq Indian healer named Elisapie met at the Baskatong Reserve in western Quebec Province, Canada. The year was 1940. Wilson spent nearly every spring and summer there for fourteen years. In addition to two Ph.Ds. he holds certification as a Reiki Master, a crystal healer, a spiritual counselor, and is certified in Qigong.

ALSO BY NORMAN W. WILSON

TEXTBOOKS

Butterflies and All That Jazz with Drs. James G. Massey and James A. Powell
Windows & Images: An Introduction to the Humanities with Drs. James G. Massey and James A. Powell
The Humanities: Contemporary Images
How to Make Moral and Ethical Decisions: A Guide

NONFICTION

Shamanism What It's All About
So You Think YOU Want to be A Buddhist?
Promethean Necessity & It's Implication for Humanity
DUH! The American Educational Disaster
The Sayings of Esaugetuh, The Master of Breath
The Shaman's Journey Through Poetry with Gavriel Navarro
Healing- The Shaman's Way
Activating Your Spirit Guides-The Shaman's Way
Shamanic Manifesting
How to Get What You Want

FICTION

The Shaman's Quest
The Shaman's Transformation
The Shaman's War
The Shaman's Genesis
The Shaman's Revelations
The Making of A Shaman

www.ingramcontent.com/pod-product-compliance
Lightning Source LLC
Chambersburg PA
CBHW061429040426
42450CB00007B/962